PSYCHOLOGY PRACTITIONER GUIDEBOOKS

EDITORS

Arnold P. Goldstein, Syracuse University
Leonard Krasner, Stanford University & SUNY at Stony Brook
Sol L. Garfield, Washington University in St. Louis

REDUCING
DELINQUENCY

Pergamon Titles of Related Interest

Apter/Goldstein YOUTH VIOLENCE: Programs and Prospects

Feindler/Ecton ADOLESCENT ANGER CONTROL: Cognitive-Behavioral Techniques

Goldstein/Keller AGGRESSIVE BEHAVIOR: Assessment and Intervention

Hollin COGNITIVE-BEHAVIORAL INTERVENTIONS WITH YOUNG OFFENDERS

Horne/Sayger TREATING CONDUCT AND OPPOSITIONAL DEFIANT DISORDERS IN CHILDREN

Oster/Caro/Eagen/Lillo ASSESSING ADOLESCENTS

Rhodes/Jason PREVENTING SUBSTANCE ABUSE AMONG CHILDREN AND ADOLESCENTS

Van Hasselt/Hersen HANDBOOK OF ADOLESCENT PSYCHOLOGY

White THE TROUBLED ADOLESCENT

Related Journals
(Free sample copies available upon request)

CHILD ABUSE AND NEGLECT
CLINICAL PSYCHOLOGY REVIEW
JOURNAL OF ANXIETY DISORDERS

REDUCING DELINQUENCY
Intervention in the Community

ARNOLD P. GOLDSTEIN
Center for Research on Aggression, Syracuse University

BARRY GLICK
New York State Division for Youth, Albany

MARY JANE IRWIN
Hillside Children's Center, Syracuse

CLAUDIA PASK-McCARTNEY
Syracuse University

IBRAHIM RUBAMA
New York State Division for Youth, Syracuse

PERGAMON PRESS
New York • Oxford • Beijing • Frankfurt
São Paulo • Sydney • Tokyo • Toronto

Pergamon Press Offices:

U.S.A.   Pergamon Press, Inc., Maxwell House, Fairview Park,
                     Elmsford, New York 10523, U.S.A.

U.K.   Pergamon Press plc, Headington Hill Hall,
                     Oxford OX3 0BW, England

PEOPLE'S REPUBLIC   Pergamon Press, Qianmen Hotel, Beijing,
OF CHINA   People's Republic of China

FEDERAL REPUBLIC   Pergamon Press GmbH, Hammerweg 6,
OF GERMANY   D-6242 Kronberg, Federal Republic of Germany

BRAZIL   Pergamon Editora Ltda, Rua Eça de Queiros, 346,
                     CEP 04011, São Paulo, Brazil

AUSTRALIA   Pergamon Press Australia Pty Ltd., P.O. Box 544,
                     Potts Point, NSW 2011, Australia

JAPAN   Pergamon Press, 8th Floor, Matsuoka Central Building,
                     1-7-1 Nishishinjuku, Shinjuku-ku, Tokyo 160, Japan

CANADA   Pergamon Press Canada Ltd., Suite 271, 253 College Street,
                     Toronto, Ontario M5T 1R5, Canada

Library of Congress Cataloging in Publication Data

Reducing delinquency.

    (Psychology practitioner guidebooks)
    Includes index.
    1. Social work with delinquents and criminals.
2. Rehabilitation of juvenile delinquents. 3. Behavior
modification. 4. Juvenile delinquents--Counseling of
I. Goldstein, Arnold P. II. Series.
HV7428.R43   1989   364.3'6'019   88-34506
ISBN 0-08-036818-2
ISBN 0-08-036817-4 (pbk.)

Printed in the United States of America

Contents

Preface   **vii**

Chapter
1   Community-Based Intervention: A Review   1

2   Aggression Replacement Training:
     Background and Procedures   17

3   The Youth Program   31

4   The Family Program   60

5   Program Evaluation   80

6   Administration of Community-Based Programs   94

7   Future Perspectives   113

References   **118**

Author Index   **125**

Subject Index   **129**

About the Authors   **131**

Series List   **133**

Preface

In 1983, we developed and began evaluating Aggression Replacement Training, a multimodal intervention designed to alter the behavior of delinquent youth. Its constituent procedures focused upon psychological skills, anger control, and moral reasoning as the specific targets for change. The initial evaluation efforts were aimed at incarcerated youth and yielded quite promising results: psychological skills were enhanced, anger and aggression were reduced, and levels of moral reasoning rose. Encouraged by these results, we then developed the project described in this book. This project extends our earlier efforts to youth in aftercare, currently living in community settings. The goal of the project is to examine the effectiveness of Aggression Replacement Training, not for institutional adjustment, but for its immediate and longer-term impact on functioning within the community. Thus, outcome criteria include not only proximal matters of skill acquisition and anger control, but the distal and consequential matter of recidivism.

There is a second, equally important focus of this project. Many psychological intervention efforts in recent years have been increasingly systemic or ecological in their thrust, and ours is no exception. In addition to its primary focus on intervening for delinquent youth, we have offered and evaluted Aggression Replacement Training provided to key family members such as parents and siblings. Our prediction is that, whatever the effects of Aggression Replacement Training directed to youth only, such effects are substantially enhanced when also offered to members of the youth's community-based world.

We first examine previous efforts of others to intervene constructively in the lives of juvenile delinquents in community settings (chapter 1). This review includes in-depth consideration of the efforts of others to reach such youth through parents or family. Aggression Replacement

Training—its rationale, procedures, and materials—are then described in detail (chapter 2), followed by full practitioner-oriented descriptions of our applications of these procedures to this project's participating youth (chapter 3) and families (chapter 4). Program evalution procedures and results constitute chapter 5. In this chapter is described the full protocol that constituted the two-year evaluation project that is at the heart of this book, and the array of findings that constitute its outcome. Encouraged by these outcomes and by their likely impact upon the dissemination and broader use of Aggression Replacement Training, in chapter 6 we present an administrative perspective on community-based delinquency intervention, highlighting issues and policies that must be dealt with successfully before such interventions can be conducted effectively.

In the final chapter (chapter 7), we look ahead and offer two major implications of this project. Since this three-course intervention program has yielded positive results in this and its two previous evaluations, we describe a fuller, more extensive expression of the underlying belief that psychological competencies can be taught effectively. The Prepare Curriculum illustrates this expression by presenting 10 separate domains of teachable psychological competence. Finally, since our results also clearly supported the value of working with youth's families, we also describe a more extended operational version of such systems intervention, involving family, school, work, and other community figures prominent in the lives of delinquent youth. Our goal in sketching out such a "total-immersion" ecological intervention is to strongly encourage youth-care workers and researchers to move energetically and creatively in such systemic directions.

Chapter 1

Community-Based Intervention: A Review

Community-based intervention programs designed for youngsters designated as juvenile delinquents are largely a phenomenon that began in the late 1960s and early 1970s. The phenomenon arose from several converging influences. Several of these contextual and causal influences related directly to the heavy utilization of residential institutions for the incarceration of juvenile delinquents. Reliance on institutionalization as the treatment of choice for other populations, such as mentally disordered adults, began to wane significantly. During this period, the movement toward deinstitutionalization gathered strength, and nearly 800 community mental health centers were established in the United States. Thus, two precedents emerged at the same time. Sociological thinkers also began to call attention to the stigmatizing effects of the label "juvenile delinquent," and many began to call not only for deinstitutionalization for such youth, but also for diversion from the juvenile justice system altogether. Another antiincarceration influence emerging during this period was the increasingly widespread conviction that institutionally based treatments were seldom effective and for several reasons probably could not be made more effective. According to Feldman, Caplinger, and Wodarski (1983):

> . . . . the factors that interfere with effective treatment in closed correctional institutions are myriad and potent: They include severe manpower deficiencies, multiple and conflicting organizational goals, overpopulation and accompanying social control problems, prisonization, the emergence of negative inmate sub-cultures, homogenization of inmate populations, adverse labelling and stigmatization, inadequate generalization and stabilization of desired behavior changes, and finally, excessive cost in comparison with virtually all other treatment alternatives. (p. 26)

1

Thus, within the corrections profession and in society at large, emphasis was changing from heavy reliance on institutional treatment toward community-based intervention. This change was further buttressed by the strong emergence of environmentalist theories in sociology and social learning theory in psychology. In both of these disciplines, a systems view of both causation and intervention became increasingly popular; as not only the youth himself, but his family, peers, school, and the larger community became more and more the focus of inquiry and intervention in the life of the troubled youth.

These influences were given added impetus in 1967 by the report of the President's Commission on Law Enforcement and the Administration of Justice. This commission put forth a strong and explicit call for the development and implementation of community-based interventions for delinquent youth. The call was clearly answered by the juvenile justice profession, and many such programs were established. These included halfway houses, group homes, residential and nonresidential therapeutic communities, day treatment centers, wilderness survival programs, special classrooms, summer camps, a host of juvenile diversion programs, and, for those already incarcerated, a variety of prerelease, work release, educational release, and home furlough reentry programs. Among correctional experts, enthusiasm for such programming was high. The hope, and perhaps even the expectation, was that such intervention would avoid the negative consequences of institutional placement, and would also be more effective in altering antisocial behavior and reducing recidivism. For the most part, however, the body of evaluation studies that followed yielded a somewhat different, more modest, treatment outcome.

COMMUNITY-BASED PROGRAMS

The Community Treatment Project of the California Youth Authority was one of the earliest experimental efforts to compare a community intervention (in this case, "a period of intense community supervision") with incarceration (Stark, 1967). Results of this comparison were equivocal. For some youths, the study suggested, in-community supervision may be the optimal placement, for youths whose original offense was severe, community intervention was not superior to incarceration on recidivism criteria. Largely concurring findings emerged from a second California Youth Authority evaluation, the Community Delinquency Control Project (Pond, 1968). In this study, the nature of the community intervention employed was multifaceted and included increased general supervision; intensive individual, group, and family counseling; remedial tutoring; psychiatric and group work consultation for agents; and increased use of group home and foster home placements. Anticipating the not-uncommon outcome of subsequent evaluations of the effectiveness of community interventions, evaluators of this study (Harlow, Weber, & Wilkins, 1971) showed that

> The Community Delinquency Control Project, like the Community Treatment Project, [failed to] provide unqualified support for the thesis that management of offenders in the community is significantly *more* successful in preventing further crime than is institutionalization. However, both programs have demonstrated a more important fact: offenders not normally released to community supervision can be as safely and at least as effectively handled in intensive intervention programs without institutionalization. (p. 10)

The Provo experiment was conducted in the early 1950s (Empey & Erickson, 1972) in an attempt to examine the comparative effect on recidivism of incarceration, probation, and a nonresidential, group-oriented community intervention consisting primarily of a Guided Group Interaction program. Recidivism rates were significantly higher for the previously incarcerated youth. Empey and Lubeck (1971), however, failed to replicate this result in their Silverlake experiment. In fact, they found—as had the two California Youth Authority projects—that institutional and community interventions yielded similar recidivism outcomes. Given this outcome, one should continue to note that community intervention is less expensive in terms of all the human and economic costs noted earlier to be associated with incarceration.

These early community intervention efforts were followed by a veritable mushrooming of such programs. The specific characteristics of each program were quite varied. Some reflected nothing more than the old control-oriented spirit of incarceration simply moved to a community setting; others sought more fully to be intervention in, by, and with the community. Most programs fell somewhere in between these extremes. Some of the more noteworthy and ambitious efforts include the San Francisco Rehabilitation Project (Northern California Service League, 1968), the Positive Action for Youth Program in Flint, Michigan (Terrance, 1971), the Attention Home Program in Boulder, Colorado (Hargardine, 1968), the Philadelphia Youth Development Day Treatment Center (Wilkins & Gottfredson, 1969), the Girls' Unit for Intensive Daytime Education in Richmond, California (Post, Hicks, & Monfort, 1968), the Essexfields Rehabilitation Project in Newark, New Jersey (Stephenson & Scarpitti, 1969), the Parkland Non-Residential Group Center in Louisville, Kentucky (Kentucky Child Welfare Research Foundation, 1967), Achievement Place Teaching-Family Homes (Phillips, 1968), the Detroit Foster Homes Project (Merrill-Palmer Institute, 1971), the Case II Project (Cohen & Filipczak, 1971), the Associated Marine Institute in Jacksonville

(Center for Studies of Crime and Delinquency, 1973), the Providence Educational Center in St. Louis (Center for Studies of Crime and Delinquency, 1973), Illinois United Delinquency Intervention Services (Goins, 1977), Project New Pride in Denver (U.S. Department of Justice, 1977), the Sacramento 601 Diversion Project (Romig, 1978), LaPlaya in Ponce, Puerto Rico (Woodson, 1981), the Inner City Roundtable of Youth in New York City (Center for Studies of Crime and Delinquency, 1973), the House of Umoja in Philadelphia (Woodson, 1981), and the St. Louis Experiment (Feldman, Caplinger, & Wodarski, 1983).

Not unlike the examinations of the effectiveness of residential treatments, evaluations of many of these community-based intervention efforts conducted during the 1970s yielded negative or indeterminate results (Rutter & Giller, 1983, p. 267):

> Though the relevant literature is immense, most reviews have ended with essentially negative conclusions–'no delinquent prevention strategies can be definitely recommended' (Wright & Dixon, 1977); 'with few and isolated exceptions the rehabilitative efforts that have been reported so far have had no appreciable effect on recidivism' (Martinson, 1974); 'studies which have produced positive results have been isolated, inconsistent in their evidence, and open to so much methodological criticism that they must remain unconvincing' (Brody, 1978).

As does most intervention research, delinquency intervention research suffers from very substantial methodological faults. Much of this research involves a lack of appropriate controls, inadequate samples in both size and randomness of selection, poorly conceived and inconsistently implemented interventions, inadequate or inappropriate outcome measures, insufficient attention to minimizing threats to internal or external validity, use of inappropriate statistical analyses, inattention to follow-up measurement–a veritable rogue's gallery of experimental weaknesses. It is clear that the relevant research is weak; what is less clear is why a strong conclusion–that such interventions do not work–should follow from weak research. We hold instead that the relevant evidence, instead of being interpreted as proof of lack of effectiveness, should more parsimoniously be viewed as indeterminate, generally neither adding to nor detracting from a conclusion of effectiveness or ineffectiveness. As Fagan and Hartstone (1984, p. 208) observe, accepting the conclusion that nothing works is premature for at least two reasons: First, the evaluation research practices have many weaknesses; second, a persistent problem with many studies has been the failure of either the investigator or the clinicians involved to accurately implement the intended treatment approach. "If the treatment was not operationalized from theory, not delivered as prescribed, or incorrectly measured, even the strongest evaluation design will show 'no impact.' "

As community-based intervention programs have continued to be developed, implemented, and evaluated, the beginnings of a more guardedly optimistic view may be discerned. Many programs still yield poor results, but the qualities of those that appear to work are becoming clearer. In a 1987 meta-analysis of evaluation reports on 90 community-based interventions, Gottschalk, Davidson, Gensheimer, and Mayer (1987) conclude:

> The median intervention lasted roughly 15 weeks and involved 15 hours of contact with the youths. A picture of not particularly intense interventions seemed to emerge. . . . The most popular types of interventions were some type of service brokerage, academic support or counseling, group therapy, and/or positive reinforcement. . . . Methodologically, these studies appear to have a number of problems. Few studies measured the implementation of treatment, include data collectors blind to the experimental hypotheses, or used random assignment to treatment, and no studies included random assignment of the service deliverer. In addition, over 20 percent of the studies reported some kind of unplanned variation in the treatment. Finally, 50 percent of the studies included no control group, or had a treatment-as-usual group, making it more difficult to estimate the true strength of the intervention. (pp. 276–277)

Yet, these same authors also observe:

> . . . treatments tended to be of short duration both in terms of intensity and length. It may be that most interventions simply were not powerful enough. This last explanation seems to be supported by the data as shown by the positive correlation between ES [effect size, a standardizing index of intervention efficacy] and length of treatment. In addition, we found some evidence of experimenter effects in the positive correlation among amount of intervener and service deliverer influence and ES. . . . These findings suggest some circumstances under which community interventions with delinquents may have positive effects. If a strong treatment is used and care is taken *during* the treatment to ensure that the treatment is actually being implemented as designed, then more positive effects may emerge. . . . (p. 283)

Feldman and co-workers (1983) further augment our sense of what might constitute an increasingly effective community-based intervention:

> First, the treatment setting should be as similar as possible to the client's natural environment and, if feasible, an integral part of it. . . . It is bound to minimize client reentry problems and to maximize the likelihood that learned changes will be transferred to, and stabilize within, the client's natural environment. Second, as much as possible, clients should be able to remain in their own homes. Hence, most treatment programs should not be residential ones that require a youth to live in an institution with peers

who exhibit pronounced behavioral problems. Third, clients should receive maximum exposure to prosocial peers and minimum exposure to antisocial peers. Fourth, intervention programs should enable clients to perform conventional social roles and to assume maximum responsibility for their own successes or failures. Fifth, such programs should be situated in agencies that have stable financial support. (p. 34)

These perspectives lead us to hold a not-proven, not-disproven, less pessimistic perspective on this 25-year-long series of community-based intervention programs. We would offer the following conclusions:

1. Since essentially equivalent recidivism rates for residential and community-based interventions have consistently been reported (Bartollas, 1985; Lundman, 1984), the latter is to be preferred on grounds of humaneness and expense, except for those youth for whom the more modest supervision of probation or more severe supervision of incarceration are indicated.

2. The community intervention programs that collectively appear to be most effective are those that are intense (frequent and lengthy) in delivery, well monitored to maximize correspondence between planned and actual procedures, and most community oriented—that is, most oriented toward "the reconstruction or construction of ties between the offender and the community through maintenance of family bonds, obtaining education and employment, and finding a place for the offender in the mainstream of social life" (Harlow, et al., 1971).

3. Given this emphasis on preparation for effective and satisfying within-community functioning, it appears highly desirable that community intervention for juvenile offenders include substantial stress upon acquisition of those personal, interpersonal, cognitive, and affect-associated skills that are the building-block requisites for effective family bonding, obtaining and maintaining a job, pursuing appropriate educational goals and, more generally becoming a competent, effective individual less in need of turning to antisocial means to accomplish personal aspirations.

Thus far in this chapter, we have provided a brief historical context for community-based delinquency intervention, cited an array of representative programs, and noted the generally pessimistic view of their overall efficacy, as well as discussed our more indeterminate stance and some modestly promising conclusions regarding routes to effective intervention. Where do we go from here? How can the efficacy of community-based intervetion be substantially improved? We propose below what we believe to be two especially promising avenues: prescriptive programming, and expanded systems intervention.

Prescriptive Programming

Consistently effective community-based interventions are, in our view, likely to be treatments developed, implemented, and evaluated in the spirit and methodology of what we call *prescriptive programming* (Goldstein & Glick, 1987). We believe that this perspective, which urges differential, tailored, or individualized interventions, is an especially important future path for community-based intervention, and one that has thus far received inadequate emphasis in the delinquency research and treatment literature.

Simple to define in general terms but difficult to implement effectively, prescriptive programming recognizes that different juveniles will be responsive to different change methods. The central question in prescriptive programming with juvenile delinquents is *Which types of youth, meeting with which types of change agents, for which types of interventions will yield optimal outcomes?* The prescriptive programming runs counter to the prevailing "one-true-light" assumption underlying most intervention efforts directed toward juvenile offenders. The one-true-light assumption, the antithesis of a prescriptive viewpoint, holds that specific treatments are sufficiently powerful to override substantial individual differences and aid heterogeneous groups of patients.

Research in all fields of psychotherapy has shown the one-true-light assumption to be erroneous (Goldstein, 1978; Goldstein & Stein, 1976). Palmer (1975) has shown it to be especially in error with regard to aggressive and delinquent adolescents. Palmer responded to a review by Martinson (1974) that examined several diverse intervention efforts designed to alter the deviant behavior of juvenile offenders. Martinson (1974, p. 25) concluded in his review that, "with few and isolated exceptions, the rehabilitative efforts that have been reported so far have had no appreciable effect on recidivism," but Palmer (1975) pointed out that this conclusion was based on the one-true-light assumption. In each of the dozens of studies reviewed by Martinson, there were homogeneous subsamples of adolescents for whom the treatments under study had worked. Martinson had been unresponsive to the fact that when homogeneous subsamples are combined to form a heterogeneous, full sample, the various positive, negative, and no-change treatment outcome effects within the subsamples cancel each other out. Thus, the full sample appears no different from an untreated group. But when smaller, more homogeneous, subsamples are examined separately, many treatments do work. The task, then, is not to continue the futile pursuit of the one treatment that works for all, but instead to discern which treatments administered by which treatment providers work for whom and for whom they do not.

Both the spirit and substance of the "many-true-lights" prescriptive programming viewpoint have their roots in analogous thinking and programming in change endeavors with populations other than juvenile delinquents. In work with emotionally disturbed adults and children, for example, there is Kiesler's (1969) grid model matching treaters, treatments, and clients; Magaro's (1969) individuation of psychotherapy offered and psychotherapist offering it as a function of patient social class and premorbid personality; and our own factorial, tridifferential research schema for enhancing the development of prescriptive matches (Goldstein, 1978; Goldstein & Stein, 1976). In elementary and secondary education contexts, examples of prescriptive programming include Keller's (1966) personalized instruction; Cronbach and Snow's (1977) aptitude-treatment interactions; Hunt's (1972) matching of student conceptual level and teacher instructional style; and Klausmeier, Rossmiller, and Saily's (1977) individually guided education model.

These ample precedents, however, are not the only beginnings of concern with prescriptive programs relevant to juvenile corrections. Early research specifically targeted to juvenile delinquents also points to the value of prescriptive programming. Several early findings of successful outcomes for specific interventions with subgroups of juvenile delinquents appear to be almost serendipitous side results of studies searching for overriding, one-true-light effects, a circumstance slightly diminishing their generalizability. Nonetheless, it is worth noting the differential effectiveness of each of the two most widely used interventions with juvenile delinquents: individual and group psychotherapy.

Individual psychotherapy has been shown to be effective with highly anxious delinquent adolescents (Adams, 1962), the socially withdrawn (Stein & Bogin, 1978), those displaying at most a moderate level of psychopathic behavior (Carney, 1966; Craft, Stephenson, & Granger, 1964), and those displaying a set of characteristics summarized by Adams (1961) as "amenable." Adolescents who are more blatantly psychopathic, who manifest a low level of anxiety, or those who are "nonamenable" are appropriately viewed as poor candidates for individual psychotherapy interventions.

Many group approaches have been developed in attempts to aid delinquent adolescents. Some of the more popular have been Activity Group Therapy (Slavson, 1964), Guided Group Interaction (McCorkle, Elias, & Bixby, 1958), and Positive Peer Culture (Vorrath & Brendtro, 1974). Research demonstrates that such approaches are indeed useful for older, more sociable, and people-oriented adolescents (Knight, 1969), for those who tend to be confrontation-accepting (Warren, 1974), for the more neurotic-conflicted (Harrison & Mueller, 1964), and for the acting-out neurotic (California Department of the Youth Authority, 1967). Juveniles who are younger, less sociable, or more delinquent (Knight, 1969) or who are confrontation-avoiding (Warren, 1974) or psychopathic (Craft et al., 1964) are less likely to benefit from group interventions. Other investigations also report differentially positive results for such subsamples of delinquents receiving individual or group psychotherapy as "immature-neurotic" (Jesness, 1965), short-term rather than long-term incarceration (Bernstein & Christiansen, 1965), "conflicted" (Glaser, 1973), and those "reacting to an adolescent growth crisis" (Warren, 1974).

Other investigators, studying these and other interventions, continue to succumb to their own one-true-light beliefs and suggest or imply that their nondifferentially applied approach is an appropriate blanket prescription useful with all delinquent subtypes. Keith (1984) writes in this manner as he reviews the past and current use of psychoanalytically oriented psychotherapy with juvenile delinquents. Others assume an analogously broad, nonprescriptive stance toward group psychotherapy (Lavin, Trabka, & Kahn, 1984), family therapy (Curry, Wiencrot, & Koehler, 1984), and behavior modification. In this last instance, however, there is very substantial evidence that the sets of interventions comprising behavior modification do have very broad effectiveness, at least for the acquisition of new behaviors (Davidson & Seidman, 1974; Mayer, Gensheimer, Davidson, & Gottschalk, 1986). Yet even here—perhaps especially here—a great deal of prescriptive research remains to be done. The good results of behavior modification used as a blanket prescription offer the promise of even better outcomes if behavior modification is employed in the form of differential prescriptions. As Redner, Snellman, and Davidson (1983) observe:

> Yes, behavioral interventions with delinquent populations seem successful, particularly with program related and prosocial behaviors. However, one can neither specify optimal conditions for the behavioral treatment of delinquents nor claim that behavioral interventions are extremely successful in reducing recidivism for any length of time. This area of research has consistently omitted the experimental manipulation of such potentially important variables as the role of the change agent, participant characteristics, and setting characteristic, which would allow one to make suggestions for optimal intervention conditions. (p. 218)

The utility of the differential intervention perspective with juvenile delinquents apparently also extends appropriately to interventions that are less directly psychotherapeutic and more singularly correctional/administrative in nature. Evidence suggests that probation, for example, may yield better outcomes for adolescent offenders who are neurotic (Empey, 1969), who display a reasonable level of prosocial behavior (Garrity, 1956) or social maturity (Sealy & Banks, 1971), or who are, in the terminology of the Interpersonal Maturity System, "cultural con-

formists" (California Department of the Youth Authority, 1967). Probation appears to be a substantially less useful prescriptive intervention
when the youth is nonneurotic (Empey, 1969), manipulative (Garrity,
1956), or low in social maturity (Sealy & Banks, 1971).

Diversion from the juvenile justice system is a more recent correctional/
administrative intervention than is probation, so less opportunity has
existed for its differential utilization and examination. Yet even here, as
Gensheimer, Mayer, Gottschalk, and Davidson (1986) demonstrate in
their meta-analysis of existing studies of the efficacy of diversion, overall
results do not support its value on efficacy criteria of recidivism; self-
reported delinquency; program, academic, social, or vocational behaviors; school or work attendance; self-esteem levels; or global ratings of
adjustment. However, they explain that there may be prescriptive exceptions to these negative combined results, just as these exceptions exist
for subpopulations of delinquents receiving psychotherapy. Younger
delinquents appear to profit more from diversion than do older adolescents. Those delinquents in diversion programs for long periods change
more than those involved for shorter periods. The prescriptive programming strategy, if more fully applied here, would perhaps more discern-
ingly identify other types of youth and additional diversion program
characteristics that yield higher levels of outcome efficacy. Such a result
is obscured when adolescents of all types or programs of all types are
aggregated into large samples for overall analyses of effects.

In our exploration of prescriptive programming to this point, we have
focused on two of the three classes of variables that combine to yield
optimal prescriptions: the interventions and bt types of youth to whom
the interventions are directed. But optimal prescriptions should be tridifferential, specifying type of intervention by type of client by type of
change agent. It is this last class of variable we now briefly address.

Interventions, as received by the youths to whom they are directed,
are never identical to the procedures as specified in a textbook or treatment manual. The intervention received is as specified in a manual—as
interpreted and implemented by the change agent—as perceived and
experienced by the youth. The change agent looms large in this sequence
and, just as we have all along dismissed the idea that all delinquents are
equivalent, so too must we get beyond practices that treat all change
agents as the same. Who administers the intervention does make a
difference, an assertion for which there already exists preliminary supporting evidence in the context of administering interventions to juvenile
delinquents. Grant and Grant (1959) report finding internally oriented
change agents to be highly effective with high-maturity offenders but
detrimental to low-maturity offenders. Palmer (1973) found that
"relationship/self-expression" change agents achieved their best results

with "communicative-alert, impulsive-anxious, or verbally hostile-defensive" youths, and did least well with "dependent-anxious" ones. Change agents characterized as "surveillance/self-control" did poorly with "verbally hostile-defensive" or "defiant-indifferent" delinquents but quite well with the "dependent-anxious."

Agee (1979) reported similar optimal pairings. In her work, delinquents and the change agents responsible for them were each divided into expressive and instrumental subtypes. The expressive group contained adolescents who were overtly vulnerable, hurting, and dependent. The instrumental group contained youths who were defended against their emotions, independent, and nontrusting. Expressive staff members were defined as open with expressing their feelings and working with the feeling of others. They typically value therapy and personal growth and see this as an ongoing process personally and for the youth they treat. Unlike the expressive delinquent youngsters, however, they have resolved significant past problems and are good role models because of their ability to establish warm, rewarding interpersonal relationships. Instrumental staff members were defined as not being as comfortable with feelings as the expressive staff members were. They are more likely to be invested in getting the job done than in processing feelings and are more alert to behavioral issues. They appear self-confident, cool, and somewhat distant, which impresses the instrumental delinquent.

Agee (1979) reports evidence suggesting the outcome superiority of (1) expressive-expressive and (2) instrumental-instrumental youth-change agent pairings, a finding largely confirmed in our own examination of optimal change agent empathy levels when working with delinquent youth (Edelman & Goldstein, 1984).

Clearly, these several studies of youth, treater, and treatment differential matching are an especially promising path for future community-based intervention planning, implementation, and evaluation.

Systems Intervention

There is a clear tendency, perhaps emerging especially from the "can do" ethos prevalent in the United States, to hope for and expect to find "the big solution" to major social problems. Americans tend to seek the one breakthrough or intervention program that will wipe out poverty (e.g., the War on Poverty of the 1960s) cancer (e.g., "miracle" cures), illiteracy (e.g., a sequence of early education/stimulation interventions), hunger/malnutrition (e.g., food stamps), drug abuse (e.g., "Just Say No" campaigns) and, most certainly, aggression. The "magic bullets" variously aimed at individual and collective aggression over the past few decades have included psychotherapy, behavior modification, medication, early detection, and, in America's criminal justice system, indeterminate sentences, determinate sentences, selective incapacitation, diversion from the system altogether, and many other programs. All such magic bullets miss the effectiveness target. The hoped-for breakthrough, whether for poverty, cancer, illiteracy, hunger, drug abuse, or aggression, is exceedingly rare and less and less likely to be found as the complexity of a problem increases.

Complex problems yield only to complex solutions. We believe that every act of aggression has multiple causes. When Johnny throws a book at his teacher (or draws a knife), it is unproductive to explain such behaviors as caused by Johnny's "aggressive personality," "economic disadvantage," or other single causes. Johnny's aggressive act, as well as all other acts of aggression, grow from an array of societal and individual causes.

Table 1.1 highlights the complexity of causes as a way of indicating the parallel necessity for complexity of solutions. Although greatly underused, the philosophy expressed here has appeared elsewhere, in various other guises, during the past 20 years. The call for complexity of solution has been heard before, from the community psychologist (Heller, Price, Reinharz, Riger, Wandersman, & D'Aunno, 1984), the ecological psychologist (Moos & Insel, 1974), the environmental designer (Krasner, 1980), and the systems analyst (Plas, 1986). We ourselves once ventured into this realm, in an examination of school violence and the optimal means for its reduction (Goldstein, Apter, & Harootunian, 1984).

Table 1.1. Multiple Causes of Aggressive Behavior

Causes	Examples
Physiological predisposition	Male gender; high-arousal temperament
Cultural	Societal traditions; mores that encourage or restrain aggression
Immediate interpersonal	Parental or peer criminality; punitive, non-nurturant parenting; video, movie, live aggressive models; verbal or physical attack; absence of potential censure, or threat of retaliation
Immediate physical environment	Heat; noise; crowding; pollution; traffic; territorial invasion; personal space violation
Person qualities	Self-control; repertoire of alternative prosocial values and behaviors
Disinhibitors	Alcohol; drugs; successful aggressive models; anonymity
Presence of means/aggressive cues	Guns; knives; other weapons
Presence of potential victim	Spouse; child; elderly person; other

How might a systems intervention strategy find concrete expression in the context of community-based intervention for juvenile delinquency? We believe it is necessary to go beyond intervention *in* the community (directed at youth), and provide effective treatments *of* the community (directed at the youth's system). That is, in a manner consistent with the multiple-causation theme of Table 1.1., the systems intervention route for the enhancement of outcome efficacy in community-based interventions for juvenile delinquents would optimally include treatments directed to, or provided for, the delinquent youth's parents, siblings, peers, class-mates, teachers, employers, and others in his or her immediate and larger community. Community-based intervention must become treatment *in and of* the community.

Our own initial steps in this expanded view of systems intervention, described in chapter 4, involved the provision of Aggression Replace-ment Training for parents and siblings of delinquent youth. In the fol-lowing section, we briefly review the family systems intervention work of others. Much of the related work was stimulated originally not only by the complexity-of-causation perspective we described above, but also by the pragmatic observation that many delinquent youth who devel-oped new competencies while incarcerated often failed to transfer and maintain such gains after their release into the community. Chief among the reasons given for such failure were system nonsupport and defi-ciencies in reciprocal skills. The youth's real-world significant others were insufficiently responsive to or rewarding of his or her newly learned competencies when they were displayed, or they were themselves un-skilled in the very competencies (or their reciprocals) the youth was using or trying to use, and a rapid extinction process ensued. For these reasons, several delinquency workers have sought the remedy of training parents as skilled responders and reinforcement dispensers, as well as in the very interpersonal community functioning skills taught to the youths them-selves.

A substantial number of such parent training programs have been reported. Many of them, as Kazdin & Frame (1983) suggest, teach parents reinforcement-delivery skills, such as how and for what to deliver rein-forcement; and when to deliver and when to withhold reinforcement and so forth. Others teach parents specific interpersonal skills, such as ne-gotiation or communication techniques, as a means of establishing a family environment receptive to and reciprocal to the improved inter-personal skills of the youth. Many investigations have consistently shown that parents of aggressive, delinquent youth can be trained to effectively reward their youth's constructive behaviors (Bailey, Wolf, & Phillips, 1970; Berkowitz & Graziano, 1972; O'Dell, 1974; Pawlicki, 1970; Sloop, 1975). Especially impressive in this context is the decades-long research and development effort of Gerald Patterson and his research group (Patterson, 1971, 1974, 1976, 1979).

In the community, youth will continue to use skills learned earlier, not only when real-world figures such as parents reward them with support, praise, encouragement, and the like for doing so, but also when these persons show reciprocal or complementary skill competency. The youth who shows skill in negotiating as a means of reducing family conflict will be more likely to continue negotiating disputes when parents join in. Much the same may be said for most interpersonal skills, be they simple ones, such as listening or having a conversation, or more complex competencies, such as expressing one's feelings, dealing with an accusation, or using self-control. When others show such behaviors toward us in a clear and competent manner, we are more likely to respond in kind. As was true for training parents to be competent dispensers of reinforcement, teaching constructive interpersonal skills to parents in order to establish reciprocally positive competencies has a substantial research history, including efforts with aggressive, delinquent youth. Kifer, Lewis, Green, and Phillips (1974) provided a valuable early such investigation, in their "Training predelinquent youths and their parents to negotiate conflict situations," as did Weathers and Liberman (1975) in a similar study with delinquent youth. Both Alexander and Parsons (1973; Parsons & Alexander, 1973) and Robin and his investigative team (Bright & Robin, 1981; Robin, 1983; Robin, Kent, O'Leary, Foster, & Prinz, 1977) reported a series of studies successfully training problem-solving communication skills to adolescents and their parents experiencing significant relationship difficulties with each other.

A further, and especially relevant, series of parent training investigations has been reported by Serna, Schumaker, Hazel, and Sheldon (1986), who write:

> It seems plausible that if a parent is unable to constructively and reciprocally respond when a youth attempts to use a trained skill, aversive interaction might occur. With each successive negative interaction between family members, the probability of a youth using a new skill again within the home setting is likely to be decreased; with disuse the youth may forget parts of the skill and eventually the newly trained skills may be distinguished entirely from the youth's repertoire. One solution to this problem that might facilitate the maintenance of skills is a parent-adolescent communication program focussing on several reciprocal skills. (p. 10)

Serna et al. constituted parent groups, and, using the same training procedures employed with the youth themselves, taught the parents the skills: accepting positive feedback, accepting negative feedback, negotiation, giving instructions, facilitating problem solving, giving rationales, and teaching interactions. Both their posttest and follow-up analyses demonstrated significant skills enhancement for the participating parents, and significant benefit at both measurement points for quality of parent-youth interactions.

In our own community-based intervention efforts, we too have placed particular emphasis on parent training and have done so largely in response to the strong conviction that inadequate socialization is a major contributor to the development of delinquency, and thus that parent training can serve a substantial remedial purpose. Snyder and Patterson (1987) propose that such socialization inadequacies center on parental discipline, deficiencies in positive parenting skills, monitoring, and problem solving:

> Poor and erratic disciplinary practices contribute to the development of delinquent behavior in both a direct and indirect fashion. Parents may contribute directly to the development of antisocial behavior by failing adequately and consistently to label, track, and consequate its performance, and by modeling and reinforcing aggressive antisocial modes of problem solving and relating to other family members. . . . Discipline described as lax or neglectful, as erratic or inconsistent, and as overly harsh or punitive, are predictive of adolescent delinquency and aggression. (p. 220)
>
> Parental coldness and rejection, a lack of involvement with the child, parental passivity and neglect, and a lack of shared leisure time are predictive of delinquent behavior. Products of poor positive parenting, including a lack of family cohesion, a lack of bonding with the family, and a communication of normlessness (it is permissible to use deviant means to obtain one's ends) have also been shown to be predictive of delinquency. (p. 224)
>
> Monitoring or supervision is a construct which refers to parent's awareness of their child's peer associates, free time activities, and physical whereabouts when outside the home. . . . the parents of delinquents relative to those of nondelinquents are found to have poorer monitoring skills. (pp. 226–227)
>
> Conflict is greater in the homes of delinquents than of nondelinquents. . . . Low intimacy in communication, lack of give and take in problem solving, and spending little time in problem talk is more descriptive of the parent-child relationships of delinquents than of nondelinquents. Problem solving in delinquent families is characterized by more anger, more defensiveness, more blaming, less friendly talk, less acceptance of responsibility, less problem specification, and less solution evaluation. (p. 229)

Indeed, the content areas, dynamics, and opportunities for system intervention at the level of parent training are varied and substantial. Many of the specific deficiencies and domains enumerated above formed our teaching curriculum in the parent training program described later in this book.

SUMMARY

In this chapter we have sought to look both backward and ahead. We have described the historical context that first gave rise to community-based interventions for delinquent youth, identified specific programs, (summarized the evaluations of their efficacy), shared some recent promising outcomes, described program characteristics that increasingly seem to be the signposts of effective intervention, and emphasized both prescriptive programming and expanded systems intervention as particularly promising avenues for the framing and implementation of future community-based interventions. With these perspectives as background, we turn to a detailed description of our own community-based treatment approach, Aggression Replacement Training—its rationale, procedures, and qualities incorporated to be responsive to the promising signposts of likely effectiveness described in this chapter.

Chapter 2

Aggression Replacement Training: Background and Procedures

Adequate adjustment by youngsters to the requirements and routines of daily living with family, friends, school personnel, and others, as well as effective and satisfying functioning elsewhere in the community are, in our perspective, largely a matter of psychological skill competence. *Psychological skill competence* is a functioning level of ability to control anger and aggression when provoked, express one's feelings openly and appropriately, make and follow reasonable requests, respond constructively to failure, deal effectively with group pressure, and engage in the array of other, similar behaviors that result in generally effective and rewarding relationships with others. It is our contention that a considerable proportion of the disruptiveness, overt aggression, and other interpersonal difficulties that occur in schools, at home, at work, on the street and in other community settings are reflections of psychological skill deficiencies. Such persons, in our view, are often literally weak in or lack the knowledge and ability to ask rather than demand; negotiate, compromise, or otherwise respond appropriately to conflict rather than strike out physically; or exercise self-control in lieu of becoming highly aroused and aggressive. Furthermore, they may be deficient in the skills necessary to handle frustration or failure by regrouping and trying again; to respond effectively to the complaints, anger, instructions, or accusations of others; or to behave competently in other important personal and interpersonal arenas. A substantial body of research amply supports this view of prosocial skill deficiency as an antecedent and correlate of antisocial behavior (Freedman, Rosenthal, Donahoe, Schlundt, & McFall, 1978; Patterson, Reid, Jones, & Conger, 1975; Spence, 1981).

17

PSYCHOLOGICAL SKILL
TRAINING

In response to this skill deficiency concept of delinquency and chronic aggressiveness, several closely related approaches to psychological skill training have emerged in recent years. These approaches include Life Skills Education (Adkins, 1974), Social Skills Training (Argyle, Trower, & Bryant, 1974), AWARE: Activities for Social Development (Elardo & Cooper, 1977), Relationahip Enhancement (Guerney, 1977), Teaching Conflict Resolution (Hare, 1976), Developing Human Potential (Hawley & Hawley, 1975), Interpersonal Communication, (Heiman, 1973), Directive Teaching (Stephens, 1976), and our own Structured Learning Training (Goldstein, 1973, 1981). Each of these approaches uses some combination of social learning techniques to instruct skill-deficient youngsters in the competencies lacked. In our approach, Structured Learning Training, or Skillstreaming, small groups of chronically aggressive adolescents with shared psychological skill deficiencies are

1. Shown several examples of expert use of the behaviors constituting the skills in which they are weak or lacking (e.g., *modeling*);
2. Given several, guided opportunities to practice and rehearse these competent interpersonal behaviors (e.g., *role playing*);
3. Provided with praise, reinstruction, and related feedback on how well their role playing of the skill matched the expert model's portrayal of it (e.g., *performance feedback*); and
4. Encouraged to engage in a series of activities designed to increase the chances that skills learned in the training setting will endure and be available for use when needed in the school, home, community, institution, or other real-world setting (*transfer training*).

Modeling

Structured Learning Training requires that trainees first be exposed to expert examples of the behaviors we want them to learn. The five or six trainees constituting the structured learning group are selected according to their shared skill deficiencies. Each potentially problematic behavior is referred to as a skill. Each skill is broken down into four to six different behavioral steps, each step constituting the operational definition of the given skill. Using either live acting by the group's trainers or audiovisual modeling displays, actors portray the steps of the skill being used expertly in a variety of settings relevant to the trainee's daily life. Trainees are told to watch and listen closely to the way the actors in each vignette follow the skill's behavioral steps.

Role Playing

A brief spontaneous discussion almost invariably follows the presentation of a modeling display. Trainees comment on the steps, the actors, and very often, on how the situation or skill problem portrayed occurs in their own lives. Since our primary goal in role playing is to encourage realistic behavioral rehearsal, a trainee's statements about his or her own difficulties using the skill being taught can often develop into material for his or her role play of it. To enhance the realism of the portrayal, the main actor is asked to choose a second trainee (coactor) to play the role of the significant other person in his or her life who is relevant to the skill problem. It is of crucial importance in the role play that the main actor seek to enact the steps he or she has just seen and heard modeled.

The main actor is asked to briefly describe the real skill problem situation and the real persons involved in it with whom he or she could try these behavioral steps in real life. The coactor is called by the name of the main actor's significant other during the role play. The trainer then instructs the role player to begin. It is the trainer's main responsibility to be sure that the main actor keeps role playing and attempts to follow the behavioral steps while doing so.

The role playing is continued until all trainees in the group have had an opportunity to participate, even if all the same steps must be carried over to a second or third session. It should be noted that, while the behavioral steps of each role play in the series remain the same, the actual content can and should change from role play to role play. The skill-deficiency problem as it actually occurs, or could occur, in each trainee's real-life environment should be the content of a given role play. When completed, each trainee should be better armed to act appropriately in the given reality situation.

Performance Feedback

Upon completion of each role play, feedback is briefly given. The goals of this activity are to let the main actor know how well he or she followed the skill's steps or in what ways he or she departed from them, to explore the psychological impact of the enactment on the coactor, and to provide the main actor with encouragement to try out the role-play behaviors in real life. In these critiques, the behavioral focus of structured learning is maintained. Comments must not take the form of general evaluative comments or broad generalities, but must focus on the presence or absence of specific, concrete behaviors.

Transfer of Training

Several aspects of the structured learning sessions just described have, as their primary purpose, augmentation of the likelihood that learning in the training setting will transfer to the trainee's real-life environment.

1. *Provision of general principles.* Transfer of training has been demonstrated to be facilitated by providing trainees with general mediating principles governing successful or competent performance in training and in real-world settings. The provision of general principles to Structured Learning trainees is operationalized in our training by the presentation in verbal, pictorial, and written form of appropriate information governing skill instigation, selection, and implementation principles.

2. *Overlearning.* Overlearning is a procedure whereby learning is extended over more trials than are necessary to produce initial successful changes in the trainee's behavior. The overlearning, or repetition of successful skill enactment, in the typical Structured Learning session is substantial, with the given skill taught and its behavioral steps (1) modeled several times, (2) role-played one or more times correctly by the trainee, (3) observed live by the trainee as every other group member role-plays it, (4) read by the trainee from a chalkboard and on the Skill Card, (5) written by the trainee in his or her Trainee's Notebook, (6) practiced *in vivo* one or more times by the trainee in response to skill-oriented, intrinsically interesting stimuli introduced into his or her real-life environment.

3. *Identical elements.* In perhaps the earliest experimental concern with transfer enhancement, it was found that when there was a facilitative effect of one habit on another, it was to the extent that and because they shared identical elements. The greater the similarity of physical and interpersonal stimuli in the Structured Learning setting and the home, school, or other setting in which the skill is to be applied, the greater the likelihood of a transfer. The "real-lifeness" of Structured Learning is operationalized in several ways. These operational expressions of identical elements include (1) the representative, relevant, and realistic content and portrayal of the models, protagonists, and situations in the live modeling or modeling tapes, all designed to be highly similar to what trainees are likely to face in their daily lives; (2) the physical props used in, and the arrangement of, the role-playing setting to be similar to real-life settings; (3) the choice, coaching, and enactment of the coactors to be as similar as possible to the real-life figures they represent; (4) the manner in which the role plays themselves are conducted to be as responsive as possible to the real-life interpersonal stimuli to which the trainee will actually have to respond with the given skill; (5) the *in vivo*

homework assignments; and (6) the training of natural peer groups whenever possible.

4. *Stimulus variability.* Several studies have demonstrated that positive transfer is greater when a variety of relevant training stimuli are employed. Stimulus variability is implemented in our Structured Learning studies by use of (1) rotating group leaders across groups, (2) rotating trainees across groups, (3) having trainees re-role-play a given skill across relevant settings, and/or (5) using multiple homework assignments for each skill.

5. *Real-life reinforcement.* Agras (1967), Gruber (1971), Tharp and Wetzel (1969), and dozens of other investigators have shown that stable and enduring performance in application settings of newly learned skills is very much at the mercy of real-life reinforcement contingencies. We have found it useful to implement supplemental programs outside the Structured Learning setting to help ensure that trainees obtain the reinforcements they need and thereby maintain their new behaviors. These programs include provision for both external social reward (provided by people in the trainee's real-life enironment) and self-reward (provided by the trainee).

Our discussion thus far has focused on the pedagogy of Structured Learning—that is, on *how* the skill curriculum is taught. The curriculum itself, what skills taught, is shown in Table 2.1.

As noted earlier, each skill consists of four to six behavior steps constituting the operational definition of the given skill. It is the skill's steps, which the trainers model, and which each participating youth must role-play. The behavioral steps for four representative skills are:

Skill 2: Starting a Conversation
Steps

1. Greet the other person.
2. Make small talk.
3. Decide if the other person is listening.
4. Bring up the main topic.

Skill 19: Expressing Affection
Steps

1. Decide if you have good feelings about the other person.
2. Decide if the other person would like to know about your feelings.
3. Choose the best way to express your feelings.
4. Choose the best time and place to express your feelings.
5. Express your feelings in a friendly way.

Table 2.1. Structured Learning Skills for Adolescents

Group I.	Beginning Social Skills	
	1.	Listening
	2.	Starting a conversation
	3.	Having a conversation
	4.	Asking a question
	5.	Saying thank-you
	6.	Introducing yourself
	7.	Introducing other opeople
	8.	Giving a compliment
Group II.	Advanced Social Skills	
	9.	Asking for help
	10.	Joining in
	11.	Giving instructions
	12.	Following instructions
	13.	Apologizing
	14.	Convincing others
Group III.	Skills for Dealing with Feelings	
	15.	Knowing your feelings
	16.	Expressing your feelings
	17.	Understanding the feelings of others
	18.	Dealing with someone else's anger
	19.	Expressing affection
	20.	Dealing with fear
	21.	Rewarding yourself
Group IV.	Skill Alternatives to Aggression	
	22.	Asking permission
	23.	Sharing something
	24.	Helping others
	25.	Negotiation
	26.	Using self-control
	27.	Standing up for your rights
	28.	Responding to testing
	29.	Avoiding trouble with others
	30.	Keeping out of fights
Group V.	Skills for Dealing with Stress	
	31.	Making a complaint
	32.	Answering a complaint
	33.	Sportmanship after the game
	34.	Dealing with embarrassment
	35.	Dealing with being left out
	36.	Standing up for a friend
	37.	Responding to persuasion
	38.	Responding to failure
	39.	Dealing with contradictory messages
	40.	Dealing with an accusation
	41.	Getting ready for a difficult conversation
	42.	Dealing with group pressure
Group VI.	Planning Skills	
	43.	Deciding on something to do
	44.	Deciding on what caused a problem
	45.	Setting a goal
	46.	Deciding on your abilities
	47.	Gathering information
	48.	Ranking problems by importance
	49.	Making a decision
	50.	Concentrating on a task

Skill 24: Negotiating
Steps

1. Decide if you and the other person are having a difference of opinion.
2. Tell the other person what you think about the problem.
3. Ask the other person what he/she thinks about the problem.
4. Listen openly to his/her answer.
5. Think about why the other person might feel this way.
6. Suggest a compromise.

Skill 42: Dealing with Group Pressure
Steps

1. Think about what the group wants to do and why.
2. Decide what you want to do.
3. Decide how to tell the group what you want to do.
4. Tell the group what you have decided.

To enhance trainee motivation, each week the trainers and the trainees decide together which particular skill will be taught. Ideally, each group is led by two trainers and consists of approximately six youngsters who are demonstrably deficient in the skills to be taught. Trainers are urged to alternate tasks, with one leading a given youth's role playing and the other sitting amongst the observing trainees to deal proximally with group management. We believe that one or two Structured Learning sessions per week are optimal, as such a schedule permits trainees the

---

Name _____ Date _____
Group Leaders _____
FILL IN DURING CLASS
1. What skill will you use?
2. What are the steps for the skill?
3. Where will you try the skill?
4. With whom will you try the skill?
5. When will you try the skill?
FILL IN AFTER DOING YOUR HOMEWORK
1. What happened when you did the homework?
2. Which steps did you really follow?
3. How good a job did you do in using the skill? (Circle one.)
      Excellent   Good   Fair   Poor
4. What do you think should be your next homework assignment?

FIGURE 2.1. Homework Report 1

opportunity to complete their homework assignments (see Figure 2.1) between sessions.[1]

SKILL ACQUISITION AND TRANSFER

We have conducted psychological skill training programs by means of Structured Learning since 1970, usually as part of an ongoing evaluation of its skill acquisition (do the trainees learn it?) and skill transfer (do the trainees use it where and when it counts?) Since 1976, our research and training program has focused on aggressive and disruptive adolescents and younger children in urban secondary and elementary schools, juvenile detention centers, and a variety of community settings. The results of our extended research evaluation program, involving 20 separate investigations (Goldstein, 1981; Goldstein, Sherman, Gershaw, Sprafkin, & Glick, 1978; Goldstein, Sprafkin, Gershaw, & Klein, 1979; Goldstein & Glick, 1987), may be summarized in two broad conclusions:

1. *Skill Acquisition.* Across diverse target skills, skill acquisition is a reliable training outcome, occurring in well over 90% of Structured Learning adolescent trainees. Although pleased with this outcome, we are acutely aware of the manner in which behavioral gains demonstrable in the training context are somewhat easily accomplished, given the support, encouragement, concreteness, repetition, and relatively low threat value of the trainers and training setting. We are also aware that the more consequential outcome question pertains to trainee performance in real-world contexts.

2. *Skill Transfer.* Across diverse target skills and applied (real-world) settings, skill transfer occurs in approximately 50% of Structured Learning trainees. Two reviews of intervention outcome research (Goldstein & Kanfer, 1979; Karoly & Steffan, 1980) have indicated that, across several dozen types of training and therapy interventions, the average transfer rate on follow-up is between 15 and 20% of persons seen. The 50% rate consequent to Structured Learning is a significant improvement upon this collective base rate, although it must be underscored that this cumulative average transfer finding also means that the gains shown by half of our trainees were limited to in-session acquisition. Of special consequence, however, is the consistent manner in which skill transfer in our studies strongly tended to be a function of the level of implementation of the explicit techniques designed to enhance such transfer described above.

---

[1]An extended presentation of Structured Learning procedures appears in Goldstein et al. (1981) and in Goldstein & Glick (1987).

AGGRESSION REPLACEMENT
TRAINING

The frequent failure of transfer or maintenance of training and therapeutic gains is a common outcome not only across psychological skills training approaches, but in delinquency intervention research of many types (Goldstein & Kanfer, 1979; Karoly & Steffan, 1980; Keeley, Shemberg, & Carbonell, 1976). This not-uncommon failure of training gains to generalize across settings or time formed the primary motivation for our effort to expand our training intervention beyond Structured Learning alone to what we hoped would be a more potent training program—Aggression Replacement Training. As already noted, many other efforts designed to enhance transfer have turned outward—to parents, employers, teachers, siblings, or other benign and gain-reinforcing persons available in the trainees' real-world environments. One is seldom so fortunate with chronically aggressive, delinquent youth. Far too often, parents are indifferent or unavailable; peers are the original tutors of antisocial, not prosocial, behavior; employers are nonexistent or overly busy; teachers have written off the youngster years ago. To be sure, when and if the transfer-relevant assistance of such persons can be mobilized, one should do so energetically. Much more often, however, one is left with but a single transfer-enhancement option—working with the target youngster himself. We reasoned that, if Structured Learning (or almost any other single intervention) alone fails to provide reliable transfer outcomes, then our training intervention must be broadened and its coverage and potency increased, in a fuller effort to arm the youngster with all the tools that will allow him or her to want and be able to behave in constructive, nonaggressive, and still satisfying ways in his community functioning. With this as our guiding philosophy, we constructed and have begun evaluating a three-component training intervention, Aggression Replacement Training.

1. *Structured Learning Training.* As noted previously, Structured Learning Training is a systematic, psychoeducational intervention demonstrated by many investigations to reliably serve the purpose of teaching a 50-skill curriculum of prosocial behaviors. In addition to teaching youngsters many other target behaviors, it also teaches them behaviors they may use instead of aggression in response to provocations they may experience.

2. *Anger Control Training.* This technique was developed by Feindler and her research group (Feindler, Marriott, & Iwata, 1984; Feindler & Ecton, 1987) at Adelphi University and was based, in part, on the earlier anger control and stress-inoculation research of Novaco (1975) and

Meichenbaum (1977), respectively. In contrast to Structured Learning's goal of facilitating prosocial behavior, Anger Control Training teaches youngsters how to lower their level of anger arousal. Anger Control Training sessions utilize modeling, youth role playing, and group performance feedback procedures similar to those employed in Structured Learning. As the homework effort does in Structured Learning, Hassle Logs (Figure 2.2) are used in Anger Control Training to help tie the training to real-world events—in this instance, actual provocations the youth has experienced.

Hassle Log

Name _____ Date _____

Morning _____ Afternoon _____ Evening _____

Where were you?

Classroom	_____	Friend's house	_____	Youth Center	_____
Store	_____	Movie	_____	Car	_____
Home	_____	Park	_____	On a Job	_____
Street	_____	Outside	_____	Other	_____

What happened?

Somebody insulted me.   _____
Sombody took something of mine.   _____
Somebody told me to do something.   _____
Sombody was doing something I didn't like.   _____
I did something wrong.   _____
Somebody started fighting with me.   _____
Other: _____

Who was that somebody:

A friend ____ Parent ____ Teacher/Principal ____ Coach ____
A stranger ____ Brother/Sister ____ Girlfriend/Boyfriend ____ Other: ____

What did you do?

Hit back	_____	Told peer	_____
Ran away	_____	Ignored it	_____
Yelled	_____	Used Anger Control	_____
Cried	_____	_____
Broke something	_____	
Cursed	_____	Used Structured
Told someone	_____	Learning Skill	_____
Walked away calmly	_____	_____
Talked it out	_____	_____

How did you handle yourself?

| 1 | 2 | 3 | 4 | 5 |
| Poorly | Not soWell | Okay | Good | Great |

How angry were you?

| | Really | Moderately | Mildly angry but | Not angry |
| Burning _____ | angry _____ | angry _____ | still okay _____ | at all _____ |

FIGURE 2.2.

In a series of sessions, usually once weekly, participating youth learn a series of links in a chain of anger-control responsiveness (Figure 2.3). The first link, Triggers, is an effort to help participants identify the external events and internal self-statements that elicit anger. What provokes the youth? Having begun to master this initial concern, the youths' attention is turned to identifying the particular physiological/kinesthetic cues that let them know that it is anger, and not fear, anxiety, or any other affect, that they are experiencing. Cues of anger—tensed biceps, flushing, hair on neck standing erect, sinking stomach sensation—tend to be idiosyncratic.

Having identified the stimulus involved (Triggers) and that it *is* anger one is experiencing (Cues), youth are taught a series of effective anger-reducing techniques. In our Anger Control Training program, these include deep breathing, counting backward, imagining a peaceful scene, contemplating the long-term consequences of alternative behavioral sequelae to the anger being experienced, and the use of Reminders. Reminders are, in a sense, the opposite of internal triggers. (The latter are self-statements [explanations, instruction] that instigate heightened levels of anger.) Reminders (also explanations, instructions, and the like) are designed to lower anger arousal. Some Reminders are generic and can be used widely (e.g., "chill out," "calm down," "cool off"). Some are situation specific (e.g., "Jane didn't trip me on purpose," "she always sits at her desk in the sloppy way").

If the links described thus far are used properly, the trainee may reward himself or herself, a procedure taught as the next link. Finally,

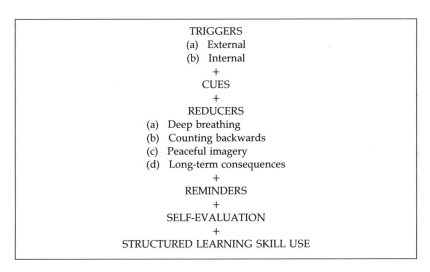

FIGURE 2.3. Anger Control Training

since Aggression Replacement Training typically involves youth attending both Structured Training and Anger Control classes every week, by the sixth or seventh week of the program, the youth is armed with a sufficient number of Structured Learning skills that he or she can complete the role playing of an anger-lowering response to a provocation by showing the group the correct thing to do instead of aggressing, namely a Structured Learning skill. By means of these components, chronically angry and aggressive youth are taught to respond to provocation (others and their own) less impulsively, more reflectively, and with less likelihood of acting-out behavior. In short, Anger Control Training teaches youngsters what *not* to do in anger-instigating situations.[2]

3. *Moral Education.* Armed with both the ability to respond to the real world prosocially, and the skills necessary to stifle or at least diminish anger, will the youngster who chronically acts out choose to do so? To enhance the likelihood that he or she will, one must enter into the realm of moral values.

When faced with the choice of behaving aggressively (usually a richly and reliably rewarded response) or prosocially (often a behavior ignored by others), the latter will be the more frequent choice the greater the youth's sense of fairness, justice, and concern for the rights of others. In a long and pioneering series of investigations, Kohlberg (1969, 1973) demonstrated that exposing youngsters to a series of moral dilemmas in a discussion-group context that includes youngsters reasoning at differing levels of moral thinking, arouses cognitive conflict whose resolution frequently advances a youngster's moral reasoning to that of the higher-level peers in the group. The dilemmas employed ideally are interesting; relevant to the world of adolescents; and involved with issues of fairness, justice, or the needs or rights of others. Examples of such dilemmas (Gibbs, 1986) are as follows:

Sam's Dilemma

Sam and his best friend, Dave, are shopping in a record store. Dave picks up a record he really likes and slips it into his backpack. Dave then walks out of the store. Moments later, the security officer and the store owner come up to Sam. The store owner says to the officer, "That's one of the boys who were stealing records!" The security officer checks Sam's backpack but doesn't find the record. "Okay, you're off the hook, but what's the name of the guy who was with you?" the officer asks Sam. "I'm almost broke because of shoplifting," the owner says. "I can't let him get away with it."

What should Sam say or do? Why? What would be the consequences?

Regina's Dilemma

"Your father called to say he had to work late," Regina's mother told her one night as they sat eating dinner. But Regina knew better. She had passed

---

[2]An extended presentation of Anger Control Training procedure appears in Feindler and Ecton (1987) and Goldstein and Glick (1987).

her father's car on the way home from school. It was parked outside the Midtown Bar and Grill. Regina's mother and father had argued many times about her father's stopping off at the bar on his way home from work. After their last argument, her father had promised he would never do it again. "Do you think I should believe your father?" Regina's mother asks her.
  What should Regina say or do? What would be the consequences?

The arousal of cognitive conflict and perspective taking necessary for the enhancement of moral reasoning is most likely to occur when a range of reasoning levels is present in the dilemma discussion group. For that reason, Aggression Replacement Training Moral Education groups typically consist of 12 members, in contrast to 6 each in Anger Control and Structured Learning Training. Trainers distribute the dilemma, read it aloud as the youths follow along, elicit a dilemma solution and its underlying reasons from each youth, rate each such response for the moral reasoning stage it reflects, and then conduct a 20- to 30-minute series of debates regarding alternative dilemma solutions between youth at adjacent moral reasoning stages until all have participated.

While moral reasoning stage advancement in youth participating in moral education is a frequent finding, efforts to utilize it by itself as a means of enhancing actual overt moral behavior have yielded mixed success (Arbuthnot & Gordon, 1983; Zimmerman, 1983). Perhaps this is because such youngsters did not have in their behavior repertoires the actual skill behaviors either for acting prosocially or for successfully inhibiting the antisocial. We thus reason that Kohlbergian Moral Education has great potential for providing constructive direction toward the prosocial and away from the antisocial in youngsters armed with the tools of both Structured Learning Training and Anger Control Training.[3]

SUMMARY

Our selection of intervention components constituting Aggression Replacement Training is based upon the nature of the behaviors or values each seeks to alter, their demonstrated success in doing so (in a training context, but with mixed success in real-world settings), and the relevance of these behaviors to the needs of chronically aggressive youngsters. There is one further, albeit somewhat more abstract, reason underlying the choice of Structured Learning Training, Anger Control Training, and Moral Education as our intervention package. We believe that interventions are successful, for transfer-enhancement purposes in particular, to the degree that they are multimodal. Behavior change may result from interventions that are explicitly targeted on overt behavior, or that seek to diminish emotional responses which inhibit use of behaviors already

---

[3]An extended presentation of the procedures of moral education appears in Goldstein and Glick (1987) and Zimmerman (1983).

in the person's behavioral repertoire, or that provide information about the consequences of alternative behaviors. Behavioral, affective, and cognitive interventions each in these differing ways possess the potential for altering overt behavior. Which alternative intervention routes, and how many of them, will correspond to any given youngster's channels of accessibility will obviously vary from youngster to youngster. We believe, however, that it generally will prove efficacious to take more than one route simultaneously. The sources and maintainers of aggression are diverse and multichannel. So, too, must its remediation be. Structured Learning Training is our *behavioral* intervention; Anger Control Training is *affective* in its substance; and Moral Education is *cognitive* in nature. Guided by our multimodal philosophy, we hold as our hypothesis that these interventions will yield outcomes superior to those resulting from single-channel interventions.

Chapter 3

The Youth Program

Earlier chapters have provided both the underlying rationale for Aggression Replacement Training (ART) and its utilization in community settings, as well as a detailed description of its specific procedures and materials. In this chapter we seek to bring the ART group to life by presenting excerpts of actual ART groups in action. ART sessions—their organization, problems, successes, failures, and more—will be described.

We also seek a second goal in this chapter. Most approaches to remediating delinquent behavior have, relatively speaking, devoted disproportionate attention to the pedagogy of the given approach (i.e., techniques, procedures, materials) and markedly insufficient attention to the second major determinant of effective outcomes: trainee motivation. In this chapter, we illustrate the diverse procedures that constitute the pedagogy of ART, but we also interweave throughout our major concern with motivating participating youth—to attend, to participate, and to utilize the lessons of ART.

THE YOUTH

Willy fidgets constantly, often lying on the table or jumping up and pounding on the walls. He twists and tugs at his T-shirt, continuously interrupting others with remarks and stories that have nothing to do with the conversation. Tremain sits apathetically but appears to listen. He seldom volunteers to perform a skill and must be constantly cajoled and encouraged by all of us. Neither Willy nor Tremain shows any interest in dating or sports. Larry and Al, on the other hand, spend most of the ART class time either talking about their sexual prowess or working on skills that emphasize their macho images. Both youths try to outshout and outboast each other, vying to be the center of attention. Sports and

31

winning are major preoccupations for both of them. Sara is a beautiful 16-year-old girl who is working two jobs and has changed high schools to get a fresh start. She has definite college plans and tries hard to get the more reluctant group members to participate. In a quiet way, she shows leadership ability, but she is somewhat unsure of herself when demonstrating it. In contrast, Elizabeth's moods sometimes disrupt the proceedings. The mother of a toddler, Elizabeth has memorized the steps to many skills and is proud to perform them properly. Suddenly, however, she flies into a rage, making accusations and swearing about other group members, and then sulks for the rest of the session. Megan is tough and doesn't care. Jerome is artistically sensitive and has amazed us with the excellence of some of his drawings. Both Megan and Jerome spend little time at home, even sleeping elsewhere most nights. Both have come to group meetings obviously high on drugs.

Twice each week, approximately six youths such as these, of differing ages, maturity levels, communication skill levels, personalities, and offenses (from attempted burglary to assault to car theft), were brought together for ART. Each of the six ART groups involved in our aftercare program was under the guidance of two cotrainers. Each group brought its own management and development problems, which surfaced throughout the four-month duration (approximately 32 meetings per group).

However, for all their differences in individual styles, participating youth often shared several qualities. They had all made mistakes in the past, had gotten caught, and had spent time in state facilities or homes for their offense. Though they were all happy to be out, most had come home to roughly the same difficult environmental circumstances each had left earlier. Peers, parents, strangers, and school figures were often negative models, or at least indifferent to positive behavior changes in our group members. Yet these youth typically expressed confidence in their ability to "handle it" vis a vis the challenges of community living. The sense of efficacy they expressed often made them reluctant to participate fully in the ART program, especially in the beginning.

THE SETTING

Youth groups met twice a week in a bright and comfortable small meeting room at the local Division for Youth office (DFY). This meeting place had both advantages and disadvantages. Because all the youth and their parents and guardians knew its location, it was convenient. But the group members often associated the office with negative feelings they had about having to "report in" once a week as part of their mandatory aftercare program. The DFY meeting place was handy for allowing trainers and youth to have an occasional informal talk with caseworkers and with the division head concerning the program's progress. But holding the ART group meetings close to the office area was often disruptive to DFY staff as well as to the other office personnel in the same building. Because of this difficulty, as well as the fact that several of the youth were attending school during the day, we chose to hold the group sessions after 5:00 p.m. Holding the meetings after office hours meant that we were relatively sure of having an available DFY staff member to transport the youth to and from the meetings in the division car. Because we quickly learned the major importance of this service in ensuring attendance, the availability of this transportation was central in our choice of meeting time.

During the later sessions of our final ART group (Group 6), we were able to experiment with two other settings for the meetings. One was a large room in a local community center that had a pleasant arrangement of living room furniture. The other was an even larger room, like an auditorium, in the upstairs of a local library. Here we had the benefit of a real stage on which to conduct role playing. Each of these locations contributed to making skill learning more realistic than it had been in the smaller office atmosphere.

ART SESSION EXCERPTS

ART procedures were described in chapter 2. In this section, we present excerpts from actual group meetings that will serve as examples of how each of the three major segments of the training—interpersonal skill training, anger control training, and moral education—were enacted by group members and cotrainers.

Trainer: Okay, Beth, how about you? What's been happening since we saw you last?

Beth: Well . . . I did have some trouble on Friday night. Every Friday my aunt and uncle come over, and my mom and her boyfriend are there, and they just sit around and have a few drinks and talk. It's nothin' I care about, so I usually go out to the house on the corner where all my friends are.

Trainer: So what made this particular Friday night different from the others?

Beth: Well, when I got my coat on to go, my mom's boyfriend started yellin' at me, and my mom and aunt and uncle all started tellin' me that I wasn't goin' anywhere and to get back in my room if I didn't want to be out there with them. But they made me sit down, and they were all saying that they don't like my friends and think that we do drugs when we are at that house.

Trainer: What did you do then, Beth?

Beth: I went into my room and picked up my radio and threw it against the wall and broke it.

Trainer: So you feel that your mom and her boyfriend and your relatives were ganging up on you, trying to force you not to see your friends, and that made you very angry?

Beth: They sure were! Yeah, I was mad!

Trainer: [*To group members*] This sounds like a situation where Beth could use one of the skills. Any suggestions on what one would be best?

Al: Dealing with Group Pressure, since there's a lot of them telling her what to do.

Trainer: How does that sound to you, Beth?

Beth: Yeah, I could try that one.

Trainer: We'll show you an example of the skill. But first, Beth, would you write the skill steps on the flip chart while we read them? [*Beth goes to the flip chart at the front of the room and begins writing.*]

Trainer: Now, everyone look on page 127 of your skill module. Al, would you please read step one; Mark, step two; Ben, step three; and Megan, step four.

Al: Think about what the group wants you to do.

Mark: Then decide what you want to do.

Ben: Then decide how to tell the group what you want to do.

Megan: Tell the group what you have decided.

Trainer: [*As Beth sits down*] Remember your step number, and watch that step as we model an example of Dealing with Group Pressure. Then, whoever reads each step can give us feedback on how well we handled that particular step in our modeling of it, just like we want you to give each other feedback when you get up to role-play this skill.

Cotrainer: I've got a good example of using this skill, but I'll need some help from everyone. Here's the situation: Three of the faculty members up at school want me to take a particular course that I already feel I know pretty well. I don't need the credits to graduate, but I am under a lot of pressure to do what these teachers tell me I should do. They have each approached me about when was I going to enroll in the class, and I have to decide what *I* think and how to deal with telling them what I have decided. So here goes!

[*Claudia and Margaret, the trainers, both go to the front of the room.*] Margaret, would you be one of the teachers talking to me about it? Remember, you already know that all of the staff have agreed that I should take the course. [*To group*] Watch for the steps!

Trainer: Claudia, have you signed up for that class we asked you to take? You're almost finished with your program and you haven't taken it like we asked you to. Some of the other faculty and I agreed that it's important, as you already know. You should know something about computers in case you are asked to teach a class in it when you graduate, you know!

Cotrainer: Okay, let's stop here for a moment. Step one says that I have to think about what the group of faculty members want me to do. *They* want me to take a particular class in computers because they think it's important for my future. Step two says that I should decide what *I* want to do. Well, I feel qualified in computers, as I have been using them for years and have taken three classes at another college before I started this program of study. I could just go along with the teachers—that would be the way they would like—but I would rather take another class of my own choosing instead! I think I would like to bargain with them. Step three says that I should decide how to tell the group. Well, I could just go ahead and take the other course that I want, and pay no attention to what they say. Then, they would certainly know my decision! Or, I could just write a petition telling them the reasons why I don't want to take the course. But I think the best way would be for me to talk to each of the faculty members, one at a time, and try to get them to agree with me that taking the course *I* want to take is just as beneficial as taking the one they want me to take. Of course, I might have to use another skill to do this, like Responding to Persuasion or Convincing Others! Okay, now I've decided to tell them—talk to each one and give good reasons about my decision. Margaret, let's show everyone what this will sound like. [Modeling continues.]

Trainer: Claudia, nice to see you again! Have you signed up for that class yet?

Cotrainer: That's what I'd like to speak to you about, Professor. Did you know that I have already taken three computer classes that cover a lot that's in the one you want me to take?

Trainer: No, I didn't. Does that mean that you think you have enough information about computer education?

Cotrainer: No, I still think I need some more, but I have a different class in mind that would be a big help to me. I was wondering if I could substitute it . . . IDE 880. It's really a more advanced class than the one you and the other teachers have requested.

Trainer: Well, that sounds all right to me. I'll talk to the others about it.

Cotrainer: Thank you, and I'll also speak to them individually about the situation. [*Modeling ends.*]

Trainer: [*To group*] How do you think Claudia did in dealing with pressure from the teachers? Al, what about skill step one?

Al: Yeah, that was good. She thought about what everyone else wanted her to do.

Beth: And she thought about *why* they wanted her to do it!

Trainer: Mark, what did you think about how well step two was done?

Mark: She did what it says . . . she decided what she wanted to do.

Trainer: Which was?

Mark: To take another class that was just as good and try to talk them into the idea.

Trainer: Step three?

Ben: That was fine, too. She decided to talk to the guys and tell them why she wanted to take another class.

Megan: Yeah, and step four was good because she went to one of the people and explained what she wanted to do and why it should be okay to do it.

Cotrainer: Thanks for the feedback. Personally, I think Margaret did a great job helping me out as coactor, and I think I handled the group pressure I was getting very well, too!

Trainer: Ready for your turn, Beth. Set the scene for us again, please.

Beth: Last Friday my aunt and uncle came over like they always do, and they were sittin' at the table with my mom and her boyfriend and havin' beers and talkin'. I was so bored, like I usually was, and got my coat on to go over to the house at the corner where my friends were. Then they started yellin' that I wasn't goin' anywhere, especially not over there. They said that those kids do drugs there.

Trainer: So you felt that they were all trying to pressure you to stay in and away from your friends, right?

Beth: They were! All of them naggin' at once. When it was just my mother there, she had let me go before and be with my friends.

Al: Hey, just go. What do you care?

Trainer: Let's let Beth make her own decision about how to handle this, Al. Does anyone remind you of your relatives or your mom or her boyfriend, so that they could help you practice this skill, Beth?

Beth: Oh, boy, let's see . . . Megan could play my aunt 'cause she has the same color hair . . . but my aunt's louder than her. [*Beth makes a nasty face.*] Margarget, you're a little bit like my mom.

Cotrainer: Why?

Beth: Because she likes to talk!

Trainer: And what about the guys? Any choices?

Beth: Oh, I don't know, anyone I guess. My uncle is mean and never listens to me, but my mom's boyfriend is okay when he's not trying' to boss me around.

Trainer: Any volunteers for those parts?

Mark: Yeah! I want to be her uncle!

Trainer: Ben, would you please try the part of Beth's mother's boyfriend? Beth says he's a type who's willing to listen sometimes but can be bossy when he wants.

Ben: [*Nods*]

Trainer: Everyone on stage! [*Youth move to the front of the room, where we arrange chairs around a "kitchen" table for all coactors. Beth is standing near them.*]

Trainer: Let's get started. Remember what Beth told you about what happened and what your character is like. Also, Mark, would you pay special attention, then you can give Beth her feedback later about her performance.

Al: Wait a minute, what are we supposed to be talkin' about while we're sittin' here?

Beth: Oh, they talk about things like hunting trips and say things about the neighbors and my other relatives.

Al: Right!

Megan: Hey! What's my name supposed to be?

Beth: You're Sue. My mom's name is Janet; her boyfriend is Bill, and my uncle's name is Jack.

Trainer: All set now? [*The "actors" answer "Yes!"*] Action!

Al: Hey, Bill, did I tell you I'm goin' hunting this weekend? I'm gonna shoot a big deer – didn't get any last year.

Megan: Shut up, Jack. That's all you ever talk about, your stupid hunting.

Ben: It's better 'n' what you two talk about [*pointing at Janet*]. All you and Janet do is gossip about the neighbors. [*Beth stands there looking convincingly bored. She goes back to her seat to get her coat, then goes back to the front of the room.*]

Al: Where the fuck are you goin', Beth?

Beth: I'm bored. I'm goin' to the corner house to see my friends.

Ben: The hell you are. You stay away from those druggies. I've been hearin' stories about that place, and you're stayin' home!

Beth: But all my friends will be there!

Margaret: Listen, Beth, if what Bill says is true, then you can't go. Go back to your room and play records or something.

Cotrainer: Okay, good group pressure. Let's stop it here for a while. Beth, let's go through the steps and see what you can do in this situation. [*Goes to the flip chart and points to step one.*] First, what does the group want you to do?

Beth: They want me to give up my friends and just stay in every night.

Cotrainer: Why? is there a reason they want you to do that?

Megan: [*Interrupts*] Yeah, they want her to stay away from drugheads, so she doesn't get into it.

Beth: Well, I guess that's the real reason, but I don't take drugs now . . . I just like to hang out with my friends. Anyway, I've never seen them doin' drugs over there. They just don't trust me or my friends.

Cotrainer: You know what they want you to do and why. Now, in step two, decide what *you* want to do.

Mark: Why don't you just go anyway?

Beth: I wanted to, that's for sure. But I don't want to be in trouble with my mom and her boyfriend all the time. I think they should understand my side.

Trainer: So you want to tell them how you feel, is that it?

Beth: Yeah. I think I'll decide to try to talk to them and tell them I'm not doin' anything wrong. Then for step three, I'll give them all the reasons that they're wrong, and tell them that I want to go see my friends.

Trainer: When will you talk to them and tell them you have decided to see your friends?

Beth: This Friday, when my aunt and uncle are there again. No, wait, I think I'll talk to mom and Bill first.

Cotrainer: Does anyone have any suggestions that Beth could use to convince her mom and the others that her decision to go over to the house is a good one?

Al: If your friends are all so great, why don't you bring 'em over to your house? Then everyone will see that hanging out with them ain't so bad, and you'll have them off your back.

Cotrainer: Could you suggest something like that when you're telling your mom and Bill what you want to do?

Beth: I can try.

Cotrainer: Now we're at step four, where you are going to tell the group what you have decided. Let's start the role play again, with Beth practicing telling her mom and Bill what she wants to do and why. You can go back to your seats, Al and Megan, and we'll let Beth talk to Margaret and Ben. [*Role play resumes.*]

Beth: You know how you told me I wasn't to go out and see my friends 'cause you were worried I'd do drugs and that they do drugs?

Ben: Yes, and we meant it, too. Your aunt and uncle agree that you should stay away from that bunch of bums!

Margaret: You listen to Bill, Beth. If you can't find other friends, then I guess you'll be stayin' in a lot of nights.

Beth: I have decided that I still want to spend time with my friends. They don't do drugs, and I don't either. We just hang out and listen to music. What if I brought some of the kids over here and you could talk to them and then you'd know it's okay for me to see them.

Margaret: All right, that sounds like a good idea. What do you think, Bill?

Ben: Sure, bring 'em over. [*Role play ends and the youth go back to their seats.*]

Trainer: Mark, since you've been sitting this one out and watching, why don't you tell Beth how you think she did on the steps?

Mark: She did fine on all of it, even though she needed a little help now and then. She ended up telling the group that she still wanted to see her friends, no matter what they thought.

Megan: Yes, but she still cared what they thought because she was going to have her mom meet her friends.

Trainer: Beth, how do you think your coactors did?

Beth: Good! Al sounded *just* like my uncle!

Trainer: And how well do you think you handled this practice dealing with the group pressure you've been getting?

Beth: I was nervous, but it wasn't as hard as I thought, so I guess I did a good job.

Cotrainer: Well, I'd say you did an excellent job. Do you think you feel ready to try this at home, with your actual family?

Beth: Well, hmmm. Maybe. Okay, I could try it and hope for the best.

Cotrainer: Good! We think you're ready, Beth. Use it if the situation arises this week, and let us know how it went. And good luck. Beth's turn is over with. Now, let's hear a situation from each of the rest of you where you have to deal with group pressure, then we'll decide who's next to role-play. Ben, what about you? Can you give us a situation?

Ben: [*Long pause*] Naw, I can't think of one.

Cotrainer: We'll come back to you, so keep thinking.

Al: I've got one, but it's different because it didn't happen yet, but I know it's gonna. There's a big party this Saturday, and I want to go, but I know there's gonna be heavy beer flowin' and my friends are gonna get drunk. I don't want to drink 'cause it only gets me in trouble. They're gonna keep pushin' me to drink, though, I know it.

Cotrainer: That one should be good to practice. Megan, what about you?

Megan: My girlfriends at school keep teasing me about one of the guys—telling me I should talk to him and ask him out, and they won't leave me alone about it.

Trainer: They're trying to pressure you into getting together with this guy?

Megan: Yeah.

Cotrainer: Mark, you've had lots of time to think about this skill.

Mark: Well, my family is trying' to tell me that I should stay in school just because they want me to be smart like them. My mother went to college and all, and she's always naggin' that I should care about school, and I'd better not drop out, and my father just goes along with her and says the same thing, practically every day. They make so much noise about it that I want to quit for sure!

Trainer: And you have your own ideas about what you want to do about school, right?

Mark: I think I do.

Cotrainer: That leaves you, Ben. Did you come up with an example of a time when you might have been pressured into something by others?

Ben: Nope.

Mark: Hey, man, we all gotta do one of these. You tellin' me that nobody ever tried to push you around?

Cotrainer: Ever had a bunch of your friends try to get you into a fight?

Ben: Yeah, sure.

Cotrainer: Well, how about telling us about one of those situations? That should fit this skill very well.

Ben: A lot of my friends talked me into jumpin' one of my cousins with them. I had to be the one to get him over to my house, then they messed his face up good.

Cotrainer: Is that what you wanted to do? Help them get your cousin?

Ben: Fuck, no. It wasn't my fight.

Cotrainer: If you go through this skill, then maybe you will be able to handle a problem like that in a better way, and not end up doing what you don't want to do just because your friends think it's a good idea. Now we know what everyone will be role-playing. Beth did a great job on her skill. Who's next?

Anger Control Training

Ray, Nick, Naomi, and Diane are present at this group session. Having already completed the Structured Learning segment of the evening's meeting, the group is now ready to move on to Anger Control Training. The youths have practiced anger control during several preceding sessions and are well versed in the techniques.

Trainer: (*To group*) Did each of you remember to be ready with a situation from your Hassle Log, where you recently got angry over something?

Naomi: I have one.

Ray: I forgot.

Trainer: Just think about a time, preferably in the last couple of days, when you blew up over an incident because someone did something that you didn't like. Naomi, why don't you start by telling us what happened to make you lose your temper.

Naomi: I had another fight with my mother.

Trainer: Tell us what started the fight.

Naomi: My mother was yellin' at my little brother, and she hit him.

Trainer: What did you do?

Naomi: I hit my mother and then I put my fist through the window and blood was spurtin' out of my wrist, so I had to go to the emergency room.

Trainer: So you ended up at the hospital. What about your mom. What happened with her?

Naomi: My mother was cryin'. That's why I have this bandage on . . . because of the glass cutting me.

Trainer: Would you rather that all that had not happened?

Naomi: Sure, but my mother just makes me furious when she goes at my little brother, and I can't stop myself from gettin' back at her.

Trainer: Thank you, Naomi. We'll get back to you soon. Anybody else got a situation?

Nick: Last night I got into a fight with my girl's old boyfriend. He was at her house—standin' out front, like he was waitin' for her to come out. Then when I came up, he started telling me to leave her alone 'cause they were getting back together. He called me a Fuckin' jerk, so I punched him in the stomach.

Trainer: Did he hit you back?

Nick: He tried to, but he didn't get me. I'm a better fighter than he is. *Nobody* gets a punch at me!

Trainer: Okay, Nick. Thanks for sharing that. Diane, what about you? Any hassles lately?

Diane: I'm gonna fight this girl at school.

Trainer: What happened between the two of you?

Diane: She and a bunch of her friends were standin' on the sidewalk when I was walkin' home – and the bitch started callin' me "nigger-lover" 'cause I only go out with black guys. I woulda' scratched her face up good right then, but there was too many of them.

Cotrainer: So you figured she was insulting you, and that made you angry. Next time she does it, somebody could get hurt, right?

Diane: You bet!

Trainer: Ray, what about you?

Ray: Well, I did get suspended from school this week. I was just sittin' there not doin' my work cause it's so boring – easy – and I keep tellin' her [the teacher] but she don't ever give me no other work to do. She screamed at me right in my face that I'm no good and in front of the class and all.

Trainer: So what did you do?

Nick: (*Laughing*) He popped her one!

Cotrainer: We'd appreciate it if you'd let Ray tell the story, Nick.

Ray: I pushed her away from my face.

Nick: Whoa-a-a-a!

Trainer: What happened when you did that?

Ray: She sent me to the principal, and he suspended me and called my Gran about it.

Trainer: Okay. It looks like we've all got some very real hassles to work on. You can each role-play your situations, and we'll see how controlling your anger when these things happened to you could have made a big difference in how things turned out for you and others involved. First, Claudia and I will give you an example of Anger Control, and then it's your turn to show us. Watch the steps [*already written on the flip chart*] as we go through them, then you can tell us how you think we did. [*Trainer and cotrainer go to the front of the room and begin to model a prepared example of Anger Control.*]

Trainer: Here's the scene: I have just started a new job a few weeks ago, and my boss, Mr. Burke, calls me in for a meeting about the work. He starts talking about what I am supposed to be doing. I look away as I am trying to get a pencil out of my purse so I can write down what he is telling me and my new schedule and all. My boss kicks my chair and says to pay attention. Believe me! I was angry. Here goes . . . [*Role play begins between trainer and cotrainer, who plays the part of the boss.*]

Cotrainer: Linda, there are a few changes in your work here that I want to discuss. First I want you to know that it will mean working some different hours, like Saturday, 7 A.M. to 2 P.M. [*Linda reaches into her purse and pulls out a pen, momentarily looking away from "Mr. Burke."*] Pay attention to me! [*Claudia, as "boss," gives Linda's chair a hard kick.*]

Trainer: I'm going to go through the Anger Control steps now, because this was the place where I got very angry. First, I think about what triggered the anger. The external trigger was my boss yelling rudely at me, changing my hours and, especially, kicking my chair. The internal trigger was my thought that he had no right to do that in any case, but especially because I was still paying attention even though I didn't look like it at that very moment. Second, I get a cue that I'm angry from my body—I catch my breath and begin to tense up. My muscles get real tight. Next, I know that I should try to stay calm, so I give myself reminders. Let's get back into role-playing the scene and I'll do the rest of the steps. [*Linda faces her "boss" again.*] Now I'm saying to myself, "Calm down. Don't make a big deal about this." So I don't do anything stupid like start telling him off, I'm going to use my anger control techniques. [*Linda is quiet for a minute.*] There . . . I have just counted slowly backward from 10, to give me time to settle down, and I've taken a few deep breaths. Next I'm going to imagine that I am not here at all, but sitting outside on my porch with a good friend, relaxing, and soaking up sunshine. [*Linda stands up, says good-bye to her "boss," and walks away. She stops to explain the fifth anger control step, Self-evaluation.*] Okay, I'm outside Mr. Burke's office, and I tell myself, "Good going, Linda. You didn't blow up, and you've still got your job."

Cotrainer: Can anyone think of a Structured Learning skill that Linda could have used with her boss after she was able to control her angry feelings?

Naomi: Standing Up for Your Rights.

Cotrainer: Great, Naomi, that's really a good suggestion. Who's next to practice?

Ray: I'll do it. (He goes to the front of the room.)

Trainer: Is that all right with all of you?

Cotrainer: I'd like to be the director on this one. Your hassle was with your teacher, as I recall, and when you blew up, you got into trouble. I would like to see how you can make things turn out diferently in this situation. Who do you want to play the part of your teacher?

Diane: Oh! Let me do it! I got a teacher just like that! [*Jumps up and goes to the front*]

Ray: Right. But you gotta be tough. You gotta be real mean about me not workin' and shout right in my face. [*Diane giggles.*]

Cotrainer: You sit in the chair, Ray, and Diane can be walking around the class and then stop when she gets to you.

Diane: [*Stops at Ray's "desk"*] You! You have been sitting here *all* day, and you haven't done a thing. I think you're just plain stupid. You can't seem to do any of the work. Why don't you just go home and stop wasting my time? [*Diane gets real close to Ray's face and breathes on him irritatingly. Ray stands up quickly and pushes her away.*]

Cotrainer: Cut! Now, Ray, you talk through the Anger Control steps on the flip chart, pretending you're at the moment when your teacher is yelling in your face.

Ray: I got angry because of what my teacher was doing . . . calling me stupid and all.

Trainer: What were you thinking at the time? You know, what was your internal trigger?

Ray: I was thinkin' that I hated her and that she was wrong because I was only not doing the work 'cause it was boring.

Trainer: How did your body feel?

Ray: Hot. And I was sick to my stomach.

Cotrainer: Let's pick up the role play again, but this time, Ray, when Diane really gets you mad, and you can feel yourself getting flushed, start following the other Anger Control steps, reminders, and reducers. [*Role play begins again, with Diane as teacher trying to make Ray as angry as she can.*]

Ray: I remind myself to chill out and forget about her. Let's see . . . then I . . . count backwards to myself . . . 10-9-8-7-6-5-4-3-2-1.

Cotrainer: Want to try some deep breathing?

Ray: I feel stupid doin' that.

Cotrainer: That's okay. If you're not comfortable with it, stick to the counting or imaging. If you had handled your anger this way, what do you think would have happened? Would you still have been suspended?

Ray: No. I would'na pushed her, I guess.

Trainer: Nick, can you think of what Ray could have said to the teacher after he calmed himself down?

Nick: No. Wait, yeah, he was being accused of being lazy, so he could have just explained what he was doing.

Trainer: Perhaps using the skill of Dealing With an Accusation. What do you think, Ray?

Ray: Uh-huh.

Cotrainer: What are you going to tell yourself, now . . . now that you successfully controlled your anger?

Ray: That I did a good job.

Cotrainer: And you did, too! What do you think, everyone, shall we give him a little applause?

Moral Education

*The Passenger Ship**

A passenger ship sank in the middle of the Atlantic. There was a great deal of panic on the ship as it became known that the ship was sinking. People were rushing into the lifeboats. The ship finally sank, and most of the people managed to get into the lifeboats.

One of the lifeboats was very overcrowded. It became evident that the boat would sink unless a number of people on it would get off. One of the passengers suggested that they take ropes and have people dragged behind the boat. However, it was winter and a person would be paralyzed if he stayed in the water for more than 10 minutes. People came up with many suggestions in order to avoid making the decision about who should live and who should die. But nobody came up with a solution that would save all the lives in the boat. After some discussion, two general opinions emerged. Some people believed that they should leave themselves to chance. What will happen will happen. They felt that it was wrong to make a decision to kill people. They might all die or all might be saved. Another

*Blatt, M., Colby, A., and Speicher, B. (1974) *Hypothetical Dilemmas for Use in Moral Discussions.* Cambridge, MA: Moral Education and Research Foundation, Harvard University.

opinion was that they should draw lots as to who should stay in the boat and who should be thrown overboard.

1. Which of these two alternatives would you see as the more justified and why? Do you have any other suggestions?
2. Do you think it is justifiable to kill a few people in order to save many?
3. Would a lottery be a fair way to make the decision? Why or why not?
4. If they decided to have a lottery but two people refused to participate, should they be allowed to abstain and stay in the boat? Why or why not?
5. Do you think there is any way to decide whose lives are the most valuable? Why or why not?

Mandy, Fraser, Juan, Shauna, and Tremain participated in this discussion under the guidance of two trainers.

Trainer: Now you've heard the dilemma we're going to be discussing. Would someone, please, give us a brief picture of what's going on?

Fraser: The ship sank and too many people got into the lifeboat. If they all stay on the boat, it will probably sink, too, so they're tryin' to figure out what to do next.

Trainer: Right. The people on the lifeboat are trying to make a decision. It is an ordinary decision?

Shauna: Well, everyone could die, that is, if they all stay there. Or at least some people could die if they draw straws or something.

Trainer: Yes. So it's not like deciding whether to visit your cousin or not, or what to wear tomorrow. It's a life-or-death decision. Is the situation clear to all of you?

Fraser: Yeah, let's get goin' here!

Trainer: Fraser, what do you think these people should do? Should they all stay on the boat and see what happens, like some people want, or should they have a lottery to decide who should get off and into the water? Or maybe you have a better idea about what they could do. Try to imagine that *you* are in the boat. Remember, it's rocking uneasily in the water because it's overloaded and waves are splashing up over the sides into the boat. It's time to decide what to do.

Fraser: If most of the people wanted a lottery, then that seems fair. I would just wait and see what most people wanted, then I would do that, too. But then, I think a lottery is a good idea because then at least some of the people would be saved. It wouldn't be good to have everyone die.

Trainer: Shauna, what about you? What do you think the people should do?

Shauna: Are there any babies in the boat?

Trainer: Possibly. Does that make a difference in your decision?

Shauna: Sure—a baby can't draw straws, so it's not fair that babies should die if their mothers have to get off the boat.

Trainer: So what do you think should be done?

Shauna: They should have a lottery so not everyone dies; but people like mothers and babies and kids should not have to do it because it wasn't their fault.

Trainer: So you think that some people are more important than others?

Shauna: Yes, and they should be saved.

Trainer: How would you decide who the most important people are?

Shauna: Like I said, the kids because they don't have anything to say about it, and . . . they're still young and haven't lived very much yet. And what if some guy is old, well he should just *have* to get off the boat. Maybe if one person is a doctor and is helping people on the boat, then he should get to stay. The rest of the people should draw straws because they're all equal.

Trainer: So you would decide on the basis of a person's value to society and to the people on the boat?

Shauna: Right.

Trainer: Tremain, have you had time to think this problem over?

Tremain: Hey, this is stupid. I'm going to stay on the boat. No matter what. If someone else wants to jump off, fine, but not me!

Trainer: So you think that you would just abstain from any decisions that the group made and do whatever you want to do. Why?

Tremain: Hey, I got a right to take care of myself. I'd beat up any guy that tried to push me out. Or, make a deal to get somebody else's straw, like— tell them I'd give their relatives money when I was saved.

Trainer: Juan, what do you think?

Juan: If I was there, I guess I would think that we should have a vote and whatever the most people said would be what I think we should do. If the most people want to stay in the boat, then we would do that. If the most people wanted a lottery, well, that's what we'd do.

Trainer: Why?

Juan: Because that's the legal way to do it. The American way. A lottery would be pretty fair, too, because then everybody would have the same chance.

Trainer: So if you were one of the people who lost and had to get off the boat, you'd still do it because you had as fair a chance as everyone else?

Juan: [*After a moment*] I guess so, but I wouldn't be so happy after I'd jumped in the water, maybe.

Trainer: Mandy, that leaves you. What do you think the people should do in this dilemma?

Mandy: Okay, I've got an idea. What if everyone talks and decides that they could take turns, some of them at a time, jumpin' off the boat and hangin' on to the side for a little while, and then getting back into the boat, and someone else can take over doin' that, too. Then at least maybe some help would come during that time. If they stay in the boat together, they'll all die, and if they have a lottery then some of them will die. With my way, they've all got a chance. Of course, the babies shouldn't have to do it, or the sick people.

Trainer: Can you explain a bit more about why your idea is best?

Mandy: Because they're all as important as each other, and no one should have to die if they use their heads and do what is best for them all.

Cotrainer: [*The cotrainer has been listening to the conversation and has made judgments on the moral reasoning stage of each of the youths' arguments. She now initiates a discussion between two youth, Tremain and Fraser, whose first responses fell at adjacent stages.*] We've got a number of different viewpoints here, although most people, with the exception of Tremain and Mandy, seem to favor the lottery decision. There are certainly a lot of different reasons for choosing that path for the people on the lifeboat. Let's get a little debate going between Tremain and Fraser. Fraser, you said that you would go along with what others decided, but that you liked the lottery idea because you think it's good that the largest number of people live. Have I got your viewpoint straight?

Fraser: Yeah, that's me all right!

Cotrainer: And Tremain, you said that you would take care of yourself and let everyone else worry about what happens to them . . . maybe even make a deal with someone so you could stay in the lifeboat, right?

Tremain: You bet . . . you got that right. I'm S-P-E-C-I-A-L!

Fraser: That's stupid, man. What make you think you're so special? Besides, you could be makin' a deal with somebody, and they'd see what a louse you were and kick you off the boat, anyway.

Tremain: Hey, I'm important, too. I got rights! I don't owe those people nothin' . . . I don't even know them. Maybe I don't even like them. They're old enough to take care of themselves.

Shauna: Except the babies or the sick people.

Fraser: If you fight to stay on the boat, everyone is gonna sit there glaring at you. Probably even *hate* you, 'cause you don't care about nobody but yourself.

Juan: [*Slouching in his chair*] Aw-w-w, his mom didn't teach him no manners.

Fraser: Nah, he just got kicked in the head, probably by some big guy on the boat. I just wouldn't want to be you sittin' there all happy and everybody thinkin' you were a Fuckin' selfish bastard.

Tremain: Well, I still don't wanna get off the boat, and besides, if I made a deal to help someone like I said — give their kids back home money or something, I would *do* it, and that wouldn't be so bad.

Cotrainer: So you're changing your mind about what you said a little bit ago, are you Tremain?

Tremain: Well-l-l, just a *little*! I still want to stay alive.

Cotrainer: What about Shauna talking to Fraser now. Try to convince Fraser that there may be things he should consider if everyone decides on a lottery and he just goes along with it.

Shauna: Maybe everyone says there should be a lottery and some baby's mother is supposed to jump into the water and freeze to death. Then what if that baby dies later because his mother is gone?

Fraser: Somebody else can look after the kid. They wouldn't just let it die . . . some other lady would do it.

Shauna: Yah? Well, maybe nobody else can feed it. And what if some of the people are hurt, and a doctor has to die. Maybe *you'd* get sick if you were there. I don't think anyone should die, either, or at least everyone should try to help each other, but some people can help more than others.

Fraser: I'm not gonna decide about that stuff, am I?

Shauna: Maybe not. But everybody knows, and the people who didn't have to go into the lottery probably wouldn't feel very good about it. But if they talked about it they would know it was for the best.

Fraser: Then everybody will choose the right thing to do, and I'll just go along with them and it will be all right, anyway!

Mandy: Well, maybe you could just care a little bit, ya know. Like think about what's goin' on and help to make the decision.

Shauna: Yeah! [*The debates continue between Juan and Shauna and between Mandy and Juan until all of the representative reasoning stage levels have been exhausted.*]

ATTENDANCE MOTIVATION

At the beginning of the ART aftercare program, we wanted to form two ART groups of approximately six youth each, to be drawn from an existing pool of 24 recently released young men and women. This proved to be a difficult and time-consuming job of locating the youth, and selling them on the potential value of ART for them. Only a few of the potential members were familiar with ART, and we had to carefully and enthusiastically explain just what the group would be doing. All of the youth were wary of being brought together for a "class" they felt would invade their personal time and newly reacquired freedom in their community.

Organizing efforts included phoning the youths (those we could locate) and describing the program and how they might benefit from it. Next, letters were sent that further explained the program and gave the date, time, and transportation arrangements provided by us for the first and subsequent meetings. This was followed by reminder phone calls on the evening before the initial meeting. When the youth could not be reached by phone, we went to their homes to talk with them. Besides relying on our own powers of persuasion, we contacted their parents or guardians and asked them to stress to their sons or daughters the importance of attending ART classes. We also enlisted the help of each youth's DFY caseworker and asked them to use their influence to encourage attendance and participation.

Despite these seemingly comprehensive efforts, early attendance did not go well, as reflected in the following trainer notes from the first session:

Group I, Session I
It is so disappointing! Willy arrived right on time, so Margaret (the cotrainer in Group I) and I spent some time talking to him, as it was 20 minutes before the next boy arrived, then another 45 minutes until Sara arrived. We had only three out of the seven who had contracted to come. Roger (the DFY driver) had gone to pick them up and the others were simply not at home, and no one seemed to know where they were. I can see how easy it is for these kids to get "lost." Now we will need to spend another couple of days chasing after those who did not show up and working on some new people from the list. With so few present, we spent all of our time just talking casually, having some doughnuts and orange juice, and telling the youth how we would have a larger group at the next meeting (we hoped!) and that then we would get into the skills training. I had wanted to do some inventory testing, but I knew the group mem-

bership was too fragile to introduce a task that some of the youth might find distasteful.

We followed the same recruitment procedures as before with potential new members, with those who did not attend, and even with those who had attended. Once again, we asked caseworkers to use their influence with the youth, this time asking that they be more forceful when stressing the importance of being in the class. All of these efforts were repeated throughout the first month of the meetings and on frequent occasions after that.

Attendance did improve. We found that if we could get the youths there a couple of times, we had other methods of encouraging them to come again. Most importantly, we worked hard at building relationships between ourselves and each group member. We spent time enthusiastically talking with them in early meetings and at the beginning of later meetings to determine personal and environmental obstacles to their use of ART skills. During these talks, we tried informally to assess each individual's interests, values, goals, and attitudes toward himself or herself and toward others. We became involved in their lives. We attended a high school football game, bought Avon products, and played table tennis against them at a local boys' club. We showed them that we cared whether or not they came to the classes, and we always asked with concern about why they had not attended one session or another.

We also created an environment that was as comfortable, warm, and trusting as we could make it. Snacks were provided for some groups on a consistent basis; for other groups, we used food as surprises to vary the routine. Group members were encouraged to bring in snacks to share with the others. Our first group even planned, on their own, to meet for Thanksgiving dinner, but we convinced them that pumpkin pie during a meeting would be sufficient! Occasionally, one of the youths asked to bring in a tape of their band or some pictures they had drawn. We always left time for these special displays after the work was finished. Confidentiality rules were established and enforced. For example, one day when we all found out that a group member had spoken to a mutual friend about what another group member had said in a session, we asked the group to use some of the skills that they had learned to firmly, but without hostility, confront the offending youth. To extend the foundation of trust we felt was essential, we ourselves shared as many personal stories as we were comfortable doing.

Building personal responsibility and commitment to the group was another significant means for increasing attendance. To do this, we simply gave the members the responsibility for being there, letting them know that we and other group members expected them to be at the meetings. These many attendance-motivating efforts were supplemented at times by extrinsic rewards. In one of our groups, we tried giving small gifts (under $10) to the person with the best attendance record. We also distributed T-shirts with an "Angerbuster" logo. All groups responded well to group celebrations of birthdays and to pizza parties at a local restaurant.

The consistent use of several of these motivational techniques seemed to make a substantial difference in attendance. The following example of a trainer's notes from one group session illustrates how some of these strategies worked in practice:

Group 1, Session 8

The meeting tonight was a joy! Three of the girls, two boys, and one friend showed up. Larry told us that Al wasn't coming, so Margaret phoned him and told him to get his running shoes on and *get here*, pretending he was running down a football field (Al *loves* football). Well, he arrived shortly thereafter! We reminded him that we expected him to attend, and if he had some kind of emergency he was to call and let us know. We started the session as usual by asking about each group member. Megan begins by telling us that she wants to be a "shrink"—a seemingly unrealistic goal, as she has just quit school. Since the subject was jobs, Sara mentioned her work at Burger King, and then she volunteered to take Willy and Elizabeth to Burger King to talk to her boss about them working there, too. A little group culture going! But if they all get jobs, what happens to the group? At least at Burger King they can arrange their schedules so they can have group evenings free most of the time.

Next, Elizabeth started talking about her recent fight with her mom. It was time to start the skills. She wanted to do the skill of Getting Ready for a Difficult Conversation. I shared a personal story in a modeling example. After all had role-played skills, we had the food break. The kids started to get a little rowdy, so we used the "pet" names we have for them to humor them into order. Larry is "Big Jock" and Sara is "Farrah Fawcett" because of her full mane of hair. More work, and then we get to the last order of business—planning the pizza party. Because we still want to keep Sara from getting bored with some of the slower members of the group, we let her lead the discussion. We got them to commit to coming next session but will still do some reminder phone calls with a couple of the boys.

Although we felt that we did everything possible to ensure the youth' presence, attendance was to remain a problem at times, in part for the following reasons.

1. Transportation did not always occur as it should. Our driver was also a full-time employee for the Division for Youth and several times was unable to pick up the participating youth because of other work commitments. When this occurred, we tried to contact the group members to let them know that the group was canceled, but as many did not have phones, this was not always possible. The trainers sometimes tried to do pickup but were seldom able to get to everyone because of having been

informed too late in the day. Even when transportation was running smoothly, some of the boys complained about being seen by their friends getting into the state car because of a "prisonlike" grid that separated the back area of the car from the front.

2. Moodiness and in-group personal differences affected motivation to attend. We had succeeded in forming closely knit groups, and disagreements sometimes escalated. Thus, if So-and-So was coming next time, So-and-So was not! In addition, other happenings in the youth's lives sometimes caused nonattendance. Absence might occur if one of the youth was having a lover's quarrel with his or her significant other, or perhaps having pressing problems with parents or relatives. Or excuses such as "I wasn't feeling up to coming" might be given. Similarly, if they were opting out of other activities in their lives, such as not attending school, they often tried to opt out of ours on that same day.

3. The youth often had good reasons for not attending. One boy's guardian had an angina attack; one of the girls had given mouth-to-mouth resuscitation to her little sister when the youngster suffered an electrical shock; a couple of our members had to help with family moves. Then there were the usual incidents of flu, job conflicts, and rehabilitation requirements scheduled for the same time as the meetings.

4. Not all attendance motivation efforts were applied consistently by cotrainers. Attempts to increase and maintain attendance were hindered when cotrainers did not contribute fully and equally in the work and when they were unwilling to dedicate some unpaid time to communicate with each other outside group hours.

When we were successful in getting the youth together, as we generally were, we still faced the problem of motivating them to participate in the Skillstreaming, Anger Control, and Moral Reasoning procedures to a level at which learning would take place.

PARTICIPATION MOTIVATION

The first two groups that we started each ran about 2 hours with a 10-minute snack break. Later, we reduced class time to an hour and a half, cutting out the break, as we found it difficult to keep the youth on a task for any longer period of time. We had contracted with the group that each member would practice two interpersonal skills of their choice from the Structured Learning Skill List, and we planned to use the rest of the session alternately practicing Anger Control or having moral-dilemma discussions. Most of the time, these plans worked quite well, although, as some of the following examples illustrate, not always.

Group 2, Session 14

Fantastic session tonight! It helped that I was well psyched up and felt full of energy again. Also, Linda (the cotrainer in Group 2) and I had been able to spend a half hour on the phone discussing what we would stress in the group. Four kids arrived via transport, and Ray was already at the DFY when we got there . . . nearly a full house.

After we got everyone quieted down, we started finding out what had been happening since we saw them last week. Ray had lost his construction job but had an interview for another job lined up; Carl had had another loud argument with his father over a piece of broken furniture; Nick and his buddy had gotten into a fist fight in the middle of the street over a girlfriend; Naomi had put her fist through a window during a family argument; according to Diane, absolutely nothing had happened to her in the last week.

Nick suggested that we do the skill of Dealing with Someone Else's Anger, and the group agreed to it, so Linda and I modeled an example, and everyone gave a current situation for the skill that they wanted to role-play. Naomi refused to take her turn, insisting that she had just made up a situation, and she never had a deal with angry people. The group pressured her loudly, and she reluctantly chose some coactors. Her role play was actually quite good. Next, we let them each choose a particular skill they wanted to act out. It was pleasing that all of the skills that were chosen all reflected dealing with their recent, very real, problems. I said that I wanted to model a skill . . . Giving a Compliment . . . then I proceeded to compliment the group on their work. Snack time was next and it was noisy, if still uneventful! Ray had brought in cookies to share, and tossed them to everyone, looking quite pleased with himself.

I then took Nick into the other room to give him our research inventories to do. He groaned about it a bit and went reluctantly. Linda and I planned to have a moral-dilemma discussion, and it had seemed appropriate because of their talkativeness this session. But because of what they had told us about the events in their lives recently, Linda stayed with the remaining four youth, and they practiced some Anger Control situations. Nick and I could hear Carl counting backwards from 10. It was not until Ray started the deep-breathing techniques for controlling anger that Nick thought he had to finish the inventories quickly so he could watch. By the close of the meeting, Linda and I had them imaging themselves on sunny beaches, or at least at their best friend's party, instead of getting angry—at least over the role-played situation.

We were happy with the session, especially since we had been a bit concerned a few weeks ago when the complexion of the group had changed, with some membership turnover because of losing some of our original members to jobs. Looks like it might work out, though!

Group 5, Session 20

As far as getting the scheduled tasks done, this was certainly one of our less productive meetings. Four out of six members showed: Mandy, Juan, Fraser, and Marty.

Even making small talk seemed to be a chore for them all tonight. They looked half asleep and bored, bored, bored. Nothing had happened to anyone lately, nobody had any problems, and everything was "just wonderful" with them . . . or so they informed us. It was obvious that Mandy and Fraser had had some kind of falling-out, however. They both sat sulking and trying too hard to ignore each other. [Mandy and Fraser had met in the group and were presently dating.] No one wanted to do the skills, and they even refused to, point-blank. This group is not especially verbal to begin with, but tonight was ridiculous.

Well, Linda and I pushed and humored them and finally simply told them the skill we would work on. Mandy and Fraser "forced" themselves to practice Expressing Your Feelings to each other. When Marty and Juan finally chose a skill, they came up with the most outrageously unrealistic situations possible. Marty had supposedly found a wallet with lots of money in it, and when he went to return it to the owner, the man wanted to give him all the money in it as a reward. Of course he wanted to use the skill of Saying Thank-You! Some wishful thinking! We reminded them that one of the rules was to try to portray each skill in the context of one of their own, real-life situations.

Group 5, Session 25

This session started out very well. Mandy and Fraser's relationship seemed stable again tonight. They both chose the skill of Understanding the Feelings of Others, and, following our modeled example, they role-played a situation with Fraser's brother in which both Fraser and Mandy felt that his brother was trying to break up their relationship. One of the other boys played the brother, and the role play really got quite heated! Both Mandy and Fraser went through the steps of the skill, explaining their separate viewpoints about how Fraser's brother might feel. Marty and Juan volunteered to try to understand each other's feelings about a mutual-one-time friend, who was now turning against them. Transportation problems had caused the group to get off to a late start, so we had time to do only one more role play each before quitting.

After much debate back and forth, the group agreed on the skill of Setting a Goal. We modeled; they role-played. Everything was going very well, especially as almost all of the youth appeared to have picked legitimate goals, such as finishing out the school year or getting a job.

Then, the evening changed dramatically! Juan asked for a bathroom key just as we were all packing up for the night. He came back into the room telling us that he had just told the building security guard to fuck himself because the man had been rude to him. We were in the process of asking him to apologize when the guard flew into our meeting place and started yelling at Juan (and us), and shoved Juan quite hard. Juan turned bright red and put up his fists. Linda and I tried to calm them both, and thank goodness it eventually worked. There were more unpleasant words as we left with the kids. All this from a boy who had looked half asleep during the latter part of the meeting.

Group 4, Session 6

There were only three youth at the beginning of the session this evening. It appeared that we would be able to give each person lots of role-play practice and still get to the moral dilemma discussion. I had also started thinking about playing some Hangman games with them if they all did their best. Twenty minutes into the meeting, Elizabeth came in with her cousin. We were just settling down again from this confusion when Mark arrived with his buddy (a person we already felt we knew because of some of Mark's role-played situations). Now we had a total of seven present.

This was not a great night to have kids straggling in this way. We had a new member, Ben, and were trying to get to know him, orient him to the group, the rules, and our activities. He appeared to be very nervous and somewhat resentful about being with us. We got the skills started again immediately. Al had a problem with two girls, both of whom he cared about, and wanted to act out the skill of Expressing Affection. Everyone came up with a situation in which they could use that skill, and the role playing began, with more than a little silliness as they acted out the parts.

Megan suddenly walked into the room, her face bright red. She sat down quietly and watched at first, but a couple of minutes later she broke into apparently uncontrollable giggling. The group began a fit of accusations and teasing about Megan being high on drugs. And she was!

There were only 20 minutes left in the session, and we had yet to finish a whole round of even *one* skill practice. Margaret (the cotrainer in Group 4) took Megan out of the room for what turned into a counseling session. I was left with a bunch of kids who had totally lost their concentration. They were extremely curious about what was happening with Megan and Margaret and, of course, everyone had to express an opinion. I tried to turn the situation into a skill practice but was only partially successful. The group was too keyed up now. Megan will definitely have a very realistic problem to role-play next group meeting, though. When Megan came back in, we had a short reminder about the rules—one of them being that no one was ever to turn up in that condition again.

I was disappointed with how I had handled the kids when I was alone with them, but seven group members is a lot for one trainer to manage alone.

Motivation to participate was deeply influenced by two dimensions of the ART program, classroom management and group development. Managing the classroom meant creating an environment in which energy expended by both trainer and trainee on problematic behavior was kept to a minimum. We strived to balance structure and freedom early on by establishing warm, friendly relationships with the youths, combined with explaining that group members had specific norms and rules to follow and that we would enforce these. While we attempted to encourage as democratic system as possible by letting the members have a significant part in making choices about what tasks we would concentrate on and by always giving them the opportunity to have a major say in choosing the particular skills they would learn, there were still evenings when we had to be more authoritative than others. A number of group development parameters seemed to aid our attempts to maintain both a smoothly running group and one in which there were high levels of trainee participation: (1) keeping the group fast paced and the youths up and moving during the role plays; (2) emphasizing a task orientation while being flexible about allowing some spontaneous chatter; (3) *not* moralizing about the past, present, or future behavior to the group members, but *suggesting* better ways to handle difficulties (usually in the form of ART skills); (4) being sensitive and responsive to any sudden changes in group moods; and (5) remaining sensitive to what a fellow cotrainer may be trying to accomplish and offering support whenever needed.

Responsiveness to the mood and flow of the group seemed especially relevant to the enhancement of participation motivation and high levels of trainee learning. The group members were much more willing to join in when they knew that the others were listening to what they were saying, that the others respected another person's problem, and that their own opinions could be expressed openly and in a pleasant manner to each other. We leaders insisted that these things happen, even though we had to spend time reminding the youth to do them. A result of this was that the group members became more knowledgeable about each other and more and more comfortable with skill role playing, anger control enactments, and moral dilemma discussion in front of each other. Cotrainers also encouraged achieving behavior to get the youths to *want* to join in by verbally praising noteworthy efforts and successes in performance, using positive achieving language such as "You can do it!" "You will do it well!" and "Give it your best try!", and by eliciting and listening enthusiastically to any success stories (within or outside of the group) that the youths shared, either spontaneously or as a part of their homework reports.

Youth also began motivating each other to participate. This appeared to occur for two reasons. First, we had set goals as to the number of skills each person must do before anybody could leave, and they were always ready to get on with other activities. Second, the youth often enjoyed the role playing and recognized its value. One girl practiced the skill of Getting Ready for a Difficult Conversation and then proceeded to tell off the whole group, stating that she was not pleased that certain group members interfered with her learning and that they had "better see how important it was to learn the skills."

Most of the youth in the six project groups came to attend sessions regularly and to participate actively over the course of the four months each group met. But a third type of trainee motivation is also relevant to the successful outcome of ART—motivation to use the competencies learned via ART in the real world.

PROSOCIAL MOTIVATION

Some attitudes the youth expressed at the beginning illustrate the challenge we faced in our efforts at enhancing prosocial motivation: "You just don't ever use the skills! I don't care what you say. If my cousin is comin' at me with a knife, I ain't gonna stand and talk to her. I'm gonna do just what I did . . . go upstairs and get a lead pipe and smack her with it." "Sometimes you just gotta hit a woman, just to show her you mean business and aren't foolin' around." "I don't help my mother when she asks me to. Why should I? She doesn't help me. She just stands there yelling and lectures me . . . telling me what to do . . . so I just start swearin.' There's no point in tryin' to convince her of anything." Indeed, the youth experienced such negativity in their daily lives that they were skeptical that they could make things better for themselves and others by behaving in more prosocial ways.

Brophy's (1985) perspective suggested to us that our own modeling behavior as trainers might be especially useful in this effort to enhance youth prosocial motivation. Brophy observes:

> Some of this socialization (such as rules for classroom conduct or for interpersonal behavior generally) is taught directly in the same way that academic content is taught. More of it, however, is communicated indirectly through modeling and other behavior that expresses teachers' beliefs, attitudes, and expectations concerning what is or is not right, just, interesting, desirable, et cetera. Consistent teacher communications on these issues will provide a direct or indirect press on students to adopt similar beliefs, attitudes, expectations, and associated behaviors. If anything, the potential for socialization effects in general and for self-fulfilling prophecy effects in particular is probably greater in the personal, social, and moral spheres than the area of academic achievement, where the possibilities open to students at a given time are limited by their intellectual abilities and present repertoires of academic knowledge and skill. (p. 183)

Staub (1979), too, points clearly to the potency of teacher or trainer behaviors and resulting group climate, as significant influences on youth motivation and learning. He comments:

> I would expect an environment in which there is reasonable structure (and effective control) that limits harmful interactions among children and encourages positive interactions, interdependence among members of the group so that cooperation and positive behavior in response to need occur naturally, a fair amount of autonomy that children are allowed so that they can learn and develop effective modes of interaction and conflict resolution, and basically democratic and just relationships between children and adults to contribute to prosocial orientation, high self-esteem, a sense of competence, role taking, and positive social behavior. (p. 254)

Thus, we set out to create a group learning experience that emphasized effective involvement with people—by both the cotrainers and the group members—whereby the youth would learn by modeling and through positive interactions within the group itself. We also wanted to establish a group environment that reinforced prosocial modes of interaction. We accomplished these goals by deliberately manipulating the group process and our own roles as leaders. First, we tried to be continuously aware of what and how we communicated information to all group members. We acted as positive role models, behaving in a caring, helping manner and overtly expressing our concern for others. When prosocial behavior was demonstrated in the group or when stories of such behavior in other settings were related, we positively reinforced these expressions through verbal praise and enthusiasm. We also tried to give empathic reactions to the youth, directed either toward them or toward another person in the situation. We also tried not to miss opportunities to elicit members' feelings about how another party involved in an interaction with them might have felt. How might a girl's mother have felt when she stormed out of the house to spend the night with a friend without calling home? How might someone's girlfriend or boyfriend have felt about being left behind at a party while their date left with someone else? At the same time, we, as cotrainers, modeled cooperative behavior with each other.

The emphasis on a democratic atmosphere was maintained. The group conflicts that inevitably arose were negotiated on the spot, as the following example illustrates:

Group 3, Session 6
    Elizabeth and Pete had another go at each other during the meeting tonight. Pete had heard that she had broken the confidentiality rules of the group, and he called her on it. Apparently, Elizabeth had told Pete's girlfriend—also a friend of Elizabeth's—that Pete said he liked another girl, too, and couldn't decide what to do, so he was dating both of them. Pete started telling her she had no business telling anybody anything that he said, and Elizabeth started flinging accusations at him . . . he was being rotten to her friend . . . he was a real jerk . . . she could say whatever she wanted to help her friend. Just as the sudden argument was getting out of hand, Elizabeth stormed out of the room and went outside. Roger (the cotrainer in Group 3) went after her and brought her back.
    As Elizabeth sulked in her chair and Pete glared at her, Roger and I told them that they would have to settle this now. We asked them to choose a skill, and preferably two, that would help them resolve their differences. They chose (with little enthusiasm) Expressing Your Feelings. Both were then able to express how they felt about each other's behavior in a civil manner. The next skill for them to use—Apologizing—was suggested by James (another group member). Neither Elizabeth nor Pete entered into this skill role play with very much pleasure, but they did it, anyway! We talked as a group about how much better it feels to actually tell someone how you feel, in a nice way, than it does when you just scream, sulk, or sneak around behind someone's back. Elizabeth and Pete finally agreed with this.

We also felt it was essential to stress cooperation and interdependence in the group. Because, it was necessary for the youth to cooperate during the skill role playing, we occasionally pointed out how they had successfully completed their tasks with the help of others. We tried to communicate the theme of interdependence by asking each youth to express an opinion when decisions needed to be made, but then to be a part of a group consensus. Several times over the months during which the group met, we asked each group member to complete some action that would contribute to a communal activity. For example, when planning to execute the pizza party, we asked that one youth call all the group members to remind them (especially anyone who had not attended the meeting at which we set the date and time); one youth was to remind the driver that we would be meeting at the restaurant, someone else was given the responsibility of ordering the meal; and someone else was asked to pay the check (with money we provided) at the restaurant.

LESSONS FOR TRAINERS

We have described our attempts to motivate trainees to attend the ART meetings, to join fully into the learning activities, and to develop more prosocial attitudes and behaviors toward others. We learned some valuable lessons from these experiences.

Communicate Among Staff Members

We found that many of our problems could have been avoided or solved promptly by making sure that more of the people who had any contact with our program were well informed as to what the program was and what was expected of them. Transportation mishaps, for example, can especially be avoided through better communication. If we expected the youths to honor their commitment to us and be ready to come to the group meetings, then it was essential that we honor our agreement to be there to pick them up. More regular communication between trainers and the transportation agents might have allowed for backup transporting procedures to have been applied consistently.

In addition, good communication between cotrainers can result in better-quality teaching and well-prepared modeling examples to help trainees learn. Good communication between trainers and caseworkers, especially about who is coming to the meetings and who is not, can result in better attendance by making the caseworkers aware that they need to remind a particular youth about the group. Good communication between parents and trainers can result in a unified force being applied for the benefit of the trainers. Within the limits of confidentiality, parents should be informed of the ART program goals, receive a copy of the curricula for the three ART segments, be encouraged to support their son's or daughter's attendance at the group, and support the youth when he or she attempts to use learned skills.

Adequate Preparation Time for Starting Groups

The more time there is to prepare for beginning an ART group, the greater the number of potential obstacles that may be identified. Adequate preparation time can ensure that the staff is well trained and that the program's goals and activities are communicated to all involved—especially caseworkers, parents, and guardians. However, actual recruitment time, the time spent between contacting the kids and the first meeting, should be kept to a minimum. Don't give the youth any time to come up with excuses for not coming or to simply disappear from whatever address or phone number you have for them.

Try to communicate a caring attitude for each youth. One of our most effective techniques for getting the kids to come and participate appeared to be demonstrating that we cotrainers cared about who they were, knew what they were interested in, and respected the positive efforts they showed us. We were careful to devote a great deal of time to building good relationships with the youth, especially in the early group sessions. We continued to work to maintain these relationships, even extending ourselves to help with problems the youth were having in the community (e.g., looking for a place to live or a job) and to join them at a local Boys' Club to play Ping-Pong. Nothing devastated task accomplishment more than moralizing about the youth's past offenses or firing a barrage of "shoulds" and "should nots" at them. Instead we talked *with* the youths and modeled behaviors we wished them to develop.

Set Group Norms and Rules Early in the Program

We quickly found that, to keep the group running smoothly, norms and rules should be established and communicated at the very first session. One permanent group norm was that everything that was said in the meetings was to be treated as confidential by both trainers and group members. We mandated a specific number of task accomplishments for each person. Listening was expected. Some other group rules were discussed and chosen as a group. Although we had to remind some youth about the rules almost constantly, we continued to enforce them, and eventually, we discovered that trainees began reminding each other of them.

Negotiate the Curriculum

Giving the youth a major role in choosing which skills they would role-play was a primary motivator for participation. Occasionally, we even let them choose whether to follow the interpersonal skill training with Anger Control Training or to do a dilemma discussion. The few times that we did have to suggest a skill for someone to do, we also had to spend a long time helping him or to create a situation to role-play. When the youth were allowed to choose, they related personal, real-world problems that could be rectified by skill practice.

Be Enthusiastic

Being enthusiastic over the full four months of each group meant keeping oneself motivated. This proved particularly hard to do after an especially discouraging meeting or when we felt that the kids were labeling us "nagging parents" or "enforcers." Our energy and enthusiasm was sometimes drained by the continual effort we expended in chasing the youth or in doing last-minute transporting. We did enjoy the lesson content and we felt more and more in control of lesson presentation and outcomes, and these two factors were central to maintaining our own positive attitudes. It was also reassuring to have a cotrainer with whom to spend some time outside of class, discussing any distasteful events and their potential remedies. Humor was invaluable to trainer motivation and morale. But most of all, simply enjoying the youths, both as individuals and as a group, seems to be the best way to maintain enthusiasm during the ART classes.

Provide Tangible Rewards

Verbal praise and attention certainly worked well for us, but they worked better when they were combined with more tangible rewards. We found that when we told the group that they could win awards for attendance or for doing the most number of skills well each month, they responded positively with attending and participating behaviors. Assuring everyone that they had a pizza party lined up at the mid- and end points of the group term delighted almost all and created expectations for some pleasant group activities.

Form Mixed Gender Groups, if Possible

Our most successful learning groups by far were those that included a balance of young men and women. Attendance was better, role playing was more realistic, and the girls tended to draw out the boys who were reluctant to participate.

Provide Surprises

Providing moderate novelty was an important aspect of maintaining trainee interest. Some techniques that worked very well were to (1) vary the meeting place occasionally (including a quiet place outdoors in good weather); (2) include some social aspects (celebrations at a local restaurant gave the youths a chance to practice some of the skills they had learned); (3) create alternative presentation modes (a prepared video demonstrating positive interpersonal interactions would be especially useful); (4) encourage group members to bring a friend or relative occasionally (not only is this beneficial for trainers to learn more about a particular trainee's environment, but it can also provide learning that might be useful to others); and (5) use a camera at sessions to take pictures of the role plays, (distributing these pictures to the "stars" of the show and sharing them with each other was always interesting for both trainers and trainees).

SUMMARY

We hope this chapter has provided a deeper sense of the nature and substance of ART groups employed with delinquent youth. The participating youngsters, their organization into functioning ART groups, their resistances and successes, the challenges faced by their trainers, and some major motivational concerns have been addressed. Consistent with our emphasis on working with both the youth and important figures in the real-world community, the next chapter describes and illustrates the use of ART with the parents and other family members of our participating delinquent youth.

Chapter 4

The Family Program

INTRODUCTION

This chapter deals with teaching ART to parents and siblings of adolescent youth who are also receiving this intervention.[1] We view the involvement of family members in ART as very important in enhancing the use of ART learned by the youth. Family therapists and other family workers have long recognized the importance of involving as many family members as possible in intervention efforts to encourage healthful changes to occur. ART training for youth *and* their families contributes to this possibility. We will both describe and illustrate concerns associated with establishing parent and sibling groups, involving its participants, and conducting the actual group meetings. We seek to provide sufficient details and examples so that other ART family groups can be started and successfully run.

We use the terms *parent group* and *family group* interchangeably throughout the chapter. Because many youth do not return to their parents' home upon release from the facility but go instead to live with other relatives, we found *parent group* to be too confining a term; thus, the name *family group* evolved.

The Structured Learning skills described in this chapter are taken from the book *Changing the Abusive Parent* (Goldstein, Keller, & Erne, 1985). This is not to imply that the parents with whom we worked were abusive. This source, however, provides clusters of skills dealing with self-control, parenting, marital relations, interpersonal relations, and supplementary competencies — skills designed to function in a manner complementary to

---

[1]Constraints on available time (for the participating parents) and our concern about its impact for this age sample regarding the skills training and anger control components of ART led us to delete from the parents' meetings any moral reasoning training.

or reciprocal with the skills being taught to the delinquent youth in their own ART sessions.

Throughout this chapter, we refer to the families with whom we worked who were in need of many resources and services. Although it is probably safe to say that most families who use public sector services (such as public health services or the Divison for Youth) are socioeconomically deprived, we do not want these needs to be confused with a lack of strength in such families. Indeed we were impressed with the resilience, resourcefulness, and reservoirs of strength in the families with whom we worked as they continued to pick themselves up, crisis after crisis. The strengths of these persons and their potential for empowerment as reflected in their ability to learn new, more satisfying ways of living provided much of our motivation in working with the families described in this chapter.

GETTING STARTED

In this section we offer suggestions for how to prepare parent meetings. We discuss selecting a meeting place, choosing facilitators, deciding what to use for enhancing attendance, and recruiting families. Whenever such premeeting details are carefully attended to, actual work with the families is enhanced.

The Meeting Place

Careful thought should be given to an appropriate meeting place. Because the agency responsible for the youth's aftercare program might elicit negative feelings in the families, a building separate from that agency's facility might be ideal. Community centers or churches are often good choices. The adult meeting room ought to be informal, with chairs and perhaps a table around which members can sit. A chalkboard upon which to write the steps of the skill to be learned at the meeting is convenient but not absolutely necessary. The steps can also be written on newsprint and posted on a wall. Comfortable chairs and a room that is well lit, ventilated, and comfortable are also necessary ingredients of the meeting place. As the group continues to meet, a large working table will probably be a helpful addition. This will prove useful when working on group projects such as planning between-meeting get-togethers, sorting pictures from outings for the group's scrapbook, and working on the group's newsletter. If sibling ART groups are to be run, we suggest that the children and adult family members meet in the same building, but in rooms sufficiently separate that is ensured of its privacy.

Choosing Facilitators

Two leaders, or cofacilitators, seem best for the parent ART group, so that responsibility for each session can be shared, and so that the group is certain to have a leader even when one leader is unable to attend. It seems advantageous to have a male-female team. This allows for modeling a cooperative male-female relationship and can be particularly useful when the cofacilitators can model real-life instances when they have disagreed and worked through their dilemmas. The skills of Apologizing and Preparing for a Stressful Conversation, for example, lend themselves to such modeling. Expressing Appreciation and Expressing Affection provide still another opportunity for modeling of positive behaviors in an ongoing relationship. Viewing cooperative relationships is often a new experience for many troubled families.

Since much of the work with the families takes place outside sessions, such as when facilitators help parents deal with their crises and dilemmas, facilitators need to know what community agencies are available and also how to obtain and advocate for needed services. Examples include knowing where to refer someone for a free pregnancy test; getting an eviction notice rescinded; knowing how to apply for food stamps; advising what to do when the amount of food stamps is inexplicably cut; and dealing effectively with several other types of real-life crises. Both kinds of help—accessing and advocating—significantly enhance the lives of the participating families and help in establishing leader credibility. Although being available to help a family with many of its dilemmas is very useful, we want to caution against becoming a rescuer, someone who tries to take care of all problems for the family. This may be tempting, but it is not empowering, since families tend to become dependent on the leaders. Leaders should encourage families to do as much as they can for themselves, such as making their own phone calls for needed services. We recommend that leaders offer support and encouragement while being a resource and linker to services, but that they do not take over a problem for a family.

We also caution against becoming caught in the middle of a hassle between a family and a service provider. It is not uncommon for a family to recount the seeming unfair treatment it is receiving from a service provider and to ask for help from the group leader. The leader should be careful to get permission in the form of a release to talk with the service provider, who will undoubtedly have his or her own story of frustration in working with the family. Staying uninvolved in the anger of each is crucial to remaining effective in helping work out a dilemma, or in helping a family accept the fact that there is no palatable solution. We once worked with a family that was constantly short of food. The mother explained that, in spite of careful budgeting of her public assistance money, she simply did not have sufficient funds. After obtaining permission to talk to the public assistance worker, we found that the family had indeed done careful budgeting, as a result of financial counseling by the agency. Even though agreements were made about how money would be spent each month by the family, the actual outlay of money was quite different from the agreed-upon contract. The family needed help in understanding that it was receiving the maximum money allowed, and although the leader could sympathize that the money from public assistance probably was not enough to cover all monthly costs, financial problems would worsen as long as funds were spent on items different from what had been agreed upon in the budget contract.

We found it helpful for at least one of the leaders to be from the agency sponsoring the group, in our case the Division for Youth. It is not unusual for parents to ask why their youth was treated in a particular way (e.g., why the youth was assigned to one facility over another) or why certain agencies function as they do. One mother told us that, in one facility where her daughter was placed, the monetary allotment for personal items was substantially more generous than it was at the latest facility to which the girl had been transferred. The mother understood when it was explained that all youth are given identical yearly allowances. Because the daughter had used nearly all of her allowance at the first facility, only the remainder could be used at the facility to which she was transferred. Such questions are more apt to be asked during meeting sessions than during the week by phone to the agency.

A word about confidentiality: As leaders gain the trust of family members, confidential information about the family may well be shared. For reasons of ethics and trust, we stress the importance of *not* repeating such information. Families should know that details about their lives that they share will not be repeated to anyone without permission. Of course, it may be that endangerment situations, such as child abuse, may need to be reported. In such instances, the family should be dealt with honestly. They should be told that the information shared will need to be used, but that the leader will stick with the family, advocating and seeking help through the difficult time.

Group leaders will be called upon to assume many roles with the families: advocate, supporter, crisis intervenor, linker to services, interpreter, teacher, and more. Weekly sessions will be only a part of the work done with the families. To the extent that families experience the leaders as dependable, consistent, supportive, and available in helping them work through dilemmas and crises at any time, interest in attending the group will be enhanced.

Providing Supports

For many families, attending the group will be possible only if services are provided that remove barriers to participation. These include child care and transportation. Although free child care is crucial for families who cannot afford to hire a babysitter, it can also be used as an opportunity for teaching of Aggression Replacement Training to the children, thus further enhancing the potency of the intervention, as all family members are exposed to skill-learning opportunities.

The reader may wish to refer to *Skillstreaming the Elementary School Child* (McGinnis & Goldstein, 1984) and *Aggression Prevention Training* (Keller, Goldstein, & Wynn, 1988) for detailed suggestions in setting up and running the children's group. As these sources suggest, the use of coleaders is recommended in order to maximize learning efficiency, minimize group management problems, and cover absences of a leader. The workers leading younger child groups should possess knowledge of appropriate age-related behaviors and activities and should genuinely enjoy children.

Transportation to and from the training setting must be provided for the family members participating in ART sessions, if at all possible. Many do not own automobiles; expecting reluctant or preoccupied participants to take public transportation to meetings will often result in their nonattendance. Obtaining and maintaining a reliable transportation arrangement for our parent and sibling groups was at times problematic and, when this was the case, attendance and group functioning clearly suffered.

Recruitment of Families

Informing a family about the ART program and inviting it to join the group can be done in a number of ways. Families can be reached, for example, by letter, by phone, by personal contact from the youth's aftercare worker, or by home visit from the family group leaders. Although these means can be effective, especially when used in combination, a home visit by the group leaders may yield the greatest success. A home visit allows the leader to present himself or herself as a friend with something to offer, particularly if it turns out that the family has a pressing need for a particular service it doesn't know how to obtain. At the same time, the home visit allows the leader to observe family members on their own turf, to gain understanding of their home situation, to make note of any special services and skills they might need, and to take the first steps in building a solid group leader–group member relationship.

The home visit time can be arranged by phone; we found appointments by letter to be least effective, since some recipients might not be able to read. With some families, we found that a spontaneous home visit as a first contact by the leader was a useful procedure, with the opportunity for the parent to say that this was not a good time, and another date could be arranged. Even when an unannounced visit was inconvenient for the family, the leader at least was able to introduce himself or herself and be perceived as a nonthreatening, even helpful, figure. More often than not, our unannounced visits were successful.

Points about the parents' ART program that might be included in initially telling parents about the groups are that (1) the group is for parents of youth who have gotten into serious difficulty; (2) the group offers the opportunity to learn new, more satisfying and more effective ways of relating to their adolescent; and (3) many parents have already found the group quite helpful. A name of a parent group member (with permission, of course) or leader to call for more details might also be included.

Following is an example of how the conversation might go at the initial home visit, informing the family of the group and inviting the family's participation:

Leader: Hi, Mrs. Jones. I am Barbara Smith and I am one of the leaders of the Family Group for Youth who are or have been in a Division for Youth facility. Is this a good time for me to talk briefly with you about the group?

Mrs. J.: Yes, I have a few minutes. (Note: If this is not a good time, simply reschedule at a mutually agreeable time.)

Leader: Perhaps you have heard about our group from your son or daughter's worker at the facility or aftercare worker – but let me explain that the Division for Youth is trying to help youth and families have a successful time together when the kids come back home. That is, we know that families and youth sometimes have a rough time trying to learn to live together again when the kids come home. And families sometimes feel alone, like they are different from other families. Our group provides support for members by encouraging and helping each other. We learn people skills, like how to control our own anger, or give instructions, or respond to failure, in order to help us get along with our adolescent better. Most families who participate enjoy learning the skills and having other people they can turn to who are experiencing the same things they are.

We meet on Wednesday evenings at the Hawthorne Family Center from 6:30 to 8:30 P.M. Transportation to and from the meeting is provided, as is child care for any younger children you might have. How does that sound?

Mrs. J.: Yeah, I might give it a try. But I'm not sure about this week.

Leader: That's okay. I'd like to check back with you during the week after you've had a chance to think about what I've said. I'd also like to leave with you a newsletter put out by our family group. Would it be okay if I give your name to one of the persons in the group so he or she can call

you? That way, you can ask questions of an actual member and see what
you think. In the meantime, do you have any questions for me?

If there are no questions at that moment, the leader will want to set
up a revisit appointment. Before leaving, however, it is good to get a
rough idea about (1) whether or not child care is needed, and if so, the
number and ages of the children; (2) whether or not transportation to the
meeting is needed; and (3) whether or not the parents have any reading
difficulties.

The follow-up appointment offers the opportunity for the parents to
ask additional questions about the group, for the leader to again go over
the purposes of the group, and to extend the invitation to attend. Our
experience has been that most families express interest in attending, yet
often they do not show up for the first meeting. Sometimes a crisis
prevents people from attending, but ambivalence about attending the
group is a more likely reason for nonattendance.

Many times, a family needs to be worked with beyond the home visits
described above, and a judgment will need to be made about the time and
energy of the leaders which they have available to continue trying to
engage families in participating. In our experience, it was rare for parents
to participate after just one or two contacts. Families usually had to be
visited several times. If it seemed possible that they would participate and
the leaders had the time to invest, we stayed with them, helping with
dilemmas in their lives that prevented them from participating. As we
describe in the next section, when a family continually promises to
attend, yet doesn't, and no crisis stems to be preventing attendance, the
leader may need to have a frank and nonjudgmental discussion with the
parents and offer them the opportunity to say that they really are not
interested.

The next section, "Engaging a Family," shows how staying with a
family can lead the members toward positive participation in the group.

Engaging a Family

The initial home visit with the Wilson family found everyone at home:
Mr. Wilson sat in his easy chair watching television; Mrs. Wilson sat in
her housecoat in another living room chair, policing their three children
as they ran in and out of the house. The eldest son, Willie, age 15, was
in a state youth facility and would not be home until the first of the year.
Living at home were Sam, 12, Tonya, 10, and Brian, 6.

The worker introduced herself and gave a brief introduction of the
group, noticing that both Mr. and Mrs. Wilson looked tentative. Both said
that the group indeed sounded like a good idea, but the worker noticed

their less-than-enthusiastic tone of voice and did not force the issue of attendance.

Mr. and Mrs. Wilson shared much information that helped the worker understand them and the many stresses in their lives. Their 2-month-old daughter had died of sudden infant death syndrome less than a year ago. Mrs. Wilson was suffering from ill health and was unable to work. She counseled with a clinic psychiatrist every other week and attended a grief support group once a week to deal with the loss of the baby. Although the necessary paperwork had been submitted and she had received verbal reassurances six weeks previously that Supplemental Security Income benefits would be forthcoming, she still had not received a check.

Mr. Wilson had been released from prison within the last year and was scheduled to attend rehabilitation classes. But he had missed the beginnig classes, so he had to wait for the beginning of the next series in the fall. Meanwhile, he was unemployed and could not find a job. Because Social Services felt he was not trying hard enough to find a job, the family's public assistance check was cut back. Mrs. Wilson talked of furniture and pieces of jewelry she was selling to make ends meet. Mr. and Mrs. Wilson had already been threatened with eviction for past-due rent.

The neighborhood in which the Wilsons lived was a continuing source of stress in their lives. They cited drug dealing and prostitution as constant worries, both in terms of potential violence and as an unhealthy atmosphere in which to raise their children. A stormy relationship with the neighbors was a regular fact of life. Just the previous evening, the Wilsons had called the police to report that the neighbors were throwing raw eggs at the Wilsons' house.

The Wilson children were friendly, and Brian, the youngest, expressed an interest in attending the children's group. The first home visit ended with both Mr. and Mrs. Wilson agreeing that the group sounded like a good idea, especially for the children. The worker and the Wilsons agreed to be in touch the next week and that it would be fine for a parent member of the group to call them during that time.

The Wilsons were not home at the agreed-upon time for the next home visit. The worker slipped a note under the front door letting them know she had been there and telling them that she was sorry to have missed them and would try again. For the next several weeks, the worker was unable to contact the Wilsons. Phone calls she made during the day were unanswered. The family was never at home during the evening. When checking with the neighbors at one point, the worker was told that the Wilsons left early each morning and did not return until late at night each day.

Quite by surprise, the worker received a call one day from Mrs. Wilson, who explained that, because of tensions with the neighbors, she and Mr. Wilson made it a point to go away with the children every day. They spent time at friends' homes or went to the beach. What had precipitated the call was that school was beginning in a couple of weeks, and Mrs. Wilson was concerned that the children did not have enough serviceable clothes to wear. She wondered if the worker knew of any resources for obtaining clothes for the children. The worker was able to round up some appropriate clothing, and when delivering them, was able to catch up on what had been happening to the Wilson family. Conflicts with the neighbors had escalated so that the children were physically fighting with other children. Mrs. Wilson was glad that school was starting so that the children would not have so much time on their hands, thus lessening the possibility of hassles with the neighbors.

Mr. and Mrs. Wilson were ready now to send the children to the group, although they themselves did not want to attend at this time. They were supported in this decision, and arrangements were made to pick the children up for the meeting. Sam, Tonya, and Brian seemed to enjoy the meetings, and when Mr. and Mrs. Wilson learned of this their own intererst in participating seemed somewhat aroused. They did not commit themselves to attending, however, and were relieved to have a night away from the children once a week. The worker continued to call on Mr. and Mrs. Wilson at home to let them know of the children's progress and of other family group activities.

One afternoon during a home visit with the Wilsons, Brian came screaming into the living room. "Come quick! Sam's been beat up." Mr. Wilson jumped to his feet swearing, threatening to beat up the person responsible, all the while ripping off his shirt as if to show that he meant what he said. Mrs. Wilson seemed shocked but not surprised at the event. Turning to the worker she exclaimed, "I knew it. Now do you believe me that this is a terrible way to have to live?"

As Mr. Wilson headed outside, he seemed determined to take on whoever was responsible for Sam's plight. Outdoors, Sam lay on the sidewalk, moaning. He was bleeding. Mrs. Wilson rushed back into the house to call the police and an ambulance. At seeing Sam, Mr. Wilson became all the more outraged and began a shouting match with a neighbor he felt was responsible for putting one of the teens up to beating up Sam. The worker hung onto Mr. Wilson and in a slow, steady, yet forceful voice, coached him along in the Anger Control skills: "Take it easy," "Chill out," "If you fight with the man, you and Sam will be all the worse off," "Breath easy," she repeated calmly to him. Mr. Wilson seemed to only half-listen as he continued to swear; nonetheless, he gradually calmed down and managed to back away from fighting. Soon the police arrived, and Sam went to the hospital emergency room shaken but not seriously hurt.

Soon after this incident, both Mr. and Mrs. Wilson began attending the group along with their children. By this time, the group leader had proven herself a friend and someone who could help in time of need. In addition, the Anger Control skills seemed now to have real meaning to Mr. and Mrs. Wilson.

Although most incidents of engaging families in group participation are not quite so dramatic, we share the above experience as a way of making several points:

1.   Up-to-date addresses are a must for locating persons quickly. An area map might also be handy; every locality has its share of streets that start in one place, are interrupted or renamed at some point, only to be continued in another place. Maps can help one circumnavigate these problems.

2.   Use perseverance with a family, as long as the family is expressing even modest interest in the group. No person is going to be interested in any group if there are more basic, significant needs to be met, such as food and shelter. Helping a family obtain the services they need can be a way of establishing trust and proving one's credibility, thereby enticing the family to attend the group. Of course, you may need to decide how much you can invest in helping in these ways when a family continues to promise that it will attend the group, yet does not follow through. An honest discussion about intentions to attend meetings might be helpful, giving parents the chance to express whether they really are or are not interested in the group. If they are truly not interested, you will want to make sure they are linked with a social worker or someone who can fill the role you have been filling (i.e., helping them meet crises). We suggest that the door always be left open for future involvement in the group if a parent states that he or she is not interested at this time. In other words, welcome the parent to attend a meeting at any time in the future. It is not unusual for a parent to seem uninterested initially, only to call or show up spontaneously at a later time.

3.   Let the parents decide how much of the group they are interested in, and do not push for more. The Wilsons, for example, were initially interested only in the children's group; this changed as time went on. It may be that the social gatherings such as potluck dinners offered by the group will be the only interesting part to some parents. As long as the parents participate in an equitable way (e.g., bringing a dish to share), this might be another way for parents to slowly test the waters.

In summary, in addition to the initial home visit or phone call extending the invitation to join the group, engaging the families may require further visits to help with various dilemmas the families might be facing. This helps the leaders establish credibility and encourages the parents to trust them. Parents may still decide not to join the group; this decision should be supported, and parents should be invited to join at a later time.

THE MEETINGS

Parent ART meetings consisted of three parts: (1) review of the week, including what has happened since the last meeting and discussion of real-world use of group-based learning; (2) Structured Learning and Anger Control Training; and (3) planning of activities for group building enhancement.

At the beginning of each meeting, it is good to acknowledge any new persons and to have all group members introduce themselves to the new attendee. Group members might give their names and tell a bit about themselves. (Facilitators might want to specify what information each person is invited to share, such as address or special interests, since the specificity may be easier to deal with.)

We have found that reviewing the week is a good way to see how use of the structured learning and anger control skills learned in previous weeks went when used in real-life settings. Furthermore, as persons relate new events and experiences, facilitators have the opportunity to spot an appropriate skill for presentation this week. For example, a person might relate apprehension about having to deal with a neighbor or child's teacher, in which case Preparing for a Stressful Conversation might be spotted as the skill on which to focus that evening.

It is not uncommon for more than one person in the group to be experiencing the same type of dilemma, so one skill often fits more than one person's needs. For example, we had an instance in which several group members were experiencing evictions, and the group chose the skill Deciding on a Task and Staying with It. This proved to be helpful, as those affected were able to prioritize and focus on a goal in the midst of their crisis. In another instance, as illustrated more fully later in this chapter, several youths in the group were unusually quiet, yet everyone denied that anything in particular was new. On further exploration, it turned out that several significant events had indeed taken place. Diane related that her husband had held a gun to her head during an argument, Mary shared that she had been evicted and her landlord had thrown her belongings on the sidewalk, and Rosetta told about having been visited by Child Protective Services during the week. All three declared: "Life is full of the same old shit." Identifying Your Feelings turned out to be an appropriate skill as a way for members to name the feeling (anger, powerlessness, frustration, etc.) being experienced in order to take appropriate action to deal with the feeling.

Example 1

The following example shows how sharing events of the week proved to be the vehicle for identifying the skill for the week:

> The discussion turned toward the topic of disciplining one's children. "You have to start out right at the very beginning and let them know who's boss," offered Shirley. "Yeah, from the time these kids are old enough to understand, you gotta let them know when they're outta line," observed Inez. Ruby shared: "I used to put David over my knee so that one of my legs was over his back and the other knee was under his stomach and his fanny would be right on top and I could whip him good." "If you use a knotted towel for whippng, it don't leave marks," added Evelyn. The leader asked, "As you think back to times you have whipped or spanked your child, what would you say about your having tried other ways of getting your kid do what you wanted?" "There ain't no trying a different way—you can talk and talk and talk and these kids won't listen so you gotta whip 'em good sometimes," said Ruby.

> *Leader:* Are you saying that it's when you feel like there's no other way— like you're desperate—that you end up whipping the kid?"
> *Shirley:* "Yeah, that's it. I know I shouldn't but I sometimes end up beating the kid."
> *Leader:* "It's times like that that you wish you could control yourself and not lose it?"
> *Ruby:* "Exactly, but I don't know what to do except whip Joe sometimes."
> *Leader:* "There is something you can do differently and I'm going to demonstrate it for you right now."

> At this point, anger control training would be the appropriate session activity, first demonstrated by the leaders, then practiced by parents.

As time goes on and you feel more comfortable presenting the skills and the parents seem to be getting the hang of the skills, you will see the need in some cases for pyramiding skills. *Pyramiding* is the presenting of two skills in sequence, the second one being a logical companion to the first.

In the following example of pyramiding, you will see that group members denied they were experiencing any particular feelings in spite of some pretty heavy events having happened in their lives that week. The leader focuses on the skill Identifying and Labeling Your Emotions to help Diane, Rosetta, and Mary name their feelings of anger, powerlessness, and frustration, so they could move beyond their immobilization to Concentration on a Task and thus feel at least some power over their situations.

Example 2

It had been a difficult week for several members in the group. Although parents, when asked as a group about how things were going, mumbled that things were "kinda like usual," the leaders knew from nervous laughter and agitated talk among members before the start of the session that there was more to be said.

Leader: "So, Ann, what's been happening this week for you?"

Ann: [*Smoking her cigarette, looking downward!*] "Oh, nothin' much."

Leader: "Nothing much, huh? Can you say anything more? You seem real quiet tonight."

Ann: "Um, no, I'm okay."

Leader: "Helen, how about you? What's been happening with you and the kids this week?"

Helen: "I'm not sure what's happenin'—I don't want to talk right now—nothin' much is new, unless you call Child Protective paying a surprise visit on me this week new—actually, it's the same old crap."

Leader: "The same old crap?"

Helen: "Yeah, they don't leave me alone. I don't know who reported me this time—probably one of Bobby's teachers. I found out that Bobby tells his teachers that he has to get himself off to school by himself in the morning."

Darlene: "My God, Bobby is six by now, isn't he? That's old enough for him to get himself off to school."

Helen: "All I know is I'm sick and tired of Child Protective showing up at the door. I'm a good mother. Someone's got it in for me and I'm about to get myself a good lawyer. I'm being harassed."

Leader: "Sounds like you're a bit angry."

Helen: "Not really—I'm kind a numb. I'm used to it. Like I said before, it's the same old crap."

[*Group members become quiet and sit silently for a bit.*]

Darlene: [*Looking at the leader*] "Don't look at me! I'm tired of fighting anymore. It's just not worth it. I don't think things will ever change." [*Looks down and becomes silent*]

Leader: "Seems like you're saying a lot. But I'm confused . . ."

Darlene: "Well, unless I do what Bill wants me to do, I'm in trouble. I mean that's not new—he wants me to do what he wants when he wants. I'm sick of it but I don't know what to do. Hell, he's not even living with us anymore, but he thinks he still owns me."

Leader: "What happened this week that makes you think that?"

Darlene: "Well, last Thursday night he held a gun to my head . . . in front of Louis, no less. I'll never forgive him for doing that in front of my little boy."

Leader: "I hope you got the police involved."

Darlene: "You kiddin'? That's just it. They don't do nothin', not a damn thing. I called them one other time when he was threatenin' me and they acted like they could care less. That's what I'm sayin'. There's nothin' I can do. I don't know what to do. But I don't like Louis seeing a gun at his mother's head."

Ann: "How'd you like it if your kid saw your stuff from your apartment dumped on the sidewalk? That's what happened to me yesterday. The landlord evicted us and threw my stuff out on the sidewalk. I told my kids *I* had thrown out the stuff on the sidewalk and it was going to be picked up by the trashmen. Who gives a shit? Can you believe we've been thrown out again?"

Leader: "Where are you staying now?"

Anne: "With my mother. I've got another place lined up for us, I think."

Leader: "So what's your reaction to all this? You're acting so calm, but a lot has happened to you!"

Ann: "Oh, I don't know,. You just get used to things, I guess."

At this point, the leader stated that it sounded like some pretty powerful things had happened to group members during the week, yet the same persons were seemingly shrugging things off almost as if nothing had happened. The leader also noted that in their seeming conclusions that "You just get used to things," "Life is the same old shit," and "There's nothin' I can do," it is difficult to see that there are things that can be done.

The leader started with the skill Identifying and Labeling Your Emotions so that Darlene, Helen, and Ann were able to name their feelings of anger, powerlessness, and frustration. The leader then presented Concentrating on a Task to help each person identify at least one task on which to focus and make plans for completing, so that each could see that there was something about her situation she could do.

There may be weeks of seeming stability with the families, so that no particular skill stands out as needed. It is important to proceed with a skill presentation, nonetheless. We have found that group members are usually able to use the skill presented at some point, and participation in the skill learning is assumed whether it fits that particular week's need or not. In short, leaders will want to come prepared with a skill to present but be able to pinpoint and present a different skill if discussion seems to make clear that a different skill would be useful.

Parents may tend to talk, even ramble on and on, about events of the week. It is important for the facilitators to allow for appropriate sharing but also to get on with the meetings so that group members can learn the skills. In other words, the meetings should not be just talk sessions, but should allow for sufficient sharing so as to identify a needed skill among group members. Facilitators should acknowledge such sharings and the dilemmas or hurts they present and even offer to talk further with the person after the meeting. However, it is important for parents to be empowered, week by week, with new skills for dealing with real-life situations. Some group members may indeed need therapy, and the leaders should be prepared to refer them for it; but group sessions should not be allowed to turn into counseling sessions.

We proceed at this point with the actual presentation of the specific skill; we hope that the skill we have selected will evolve from the general sharing. If a different skill than the one the leaders originally planned is to be presented, they can call for a recess, allow parents to get some refreshments, then write on newsprint or a chalkboard the skill and steps for the evening. Leaders will also want to use this time to decide how to model the skill for presentation. Modeling by the leaders, role playing by the group members, and providing feedback are conducted by means of the ART procedures described in chapter 2. In addition, there are some special groups management matters that arise in the course of the parent group meetings.

Keeping parents on track is particularly difficult when, for example, a husband-wife team is practicing a skill involving an area of frequent difficulty between them. If the couple tends to go on tangents or if their anger typically tends to escalate, the leaders may need to coach both persons during the role play to ensure its successful completion.

Checking on efforts at home to use skills learned in the group is an important part of all ART sessions, but it may be especially valuable when leaders note particular difficulty of group members in staying on track during the role play. When the situation being practiced is difficult, and numerous errors occur during role play, the likelihood of transferring the errors to the home environment may be diminished. Additional practice and corrective feedback may be necessary, or the person should be encouraged to choose a role-play situation that is less difficult.

During the project, we encountered several group members who could not read. We tried to screen group members ahead of time (during the home visit appraising the family of the group) by asking, "Do you have a reading difficulty of any kind?" Persons usually were up front about their reading difficulties. It should not need to be pointed out that asking ahead of time saves embarrassing people in front of the group. We found it helpful to arrange the order of persons practicing the skill during the session so that a person unable to read goes last; this enables the person to become familiar with the skill and its steps, or even to memorize them, from the repetition of others ahead of him or her. Familiarity with a skill's steps is further enhanced by the feedback section of the skill practice. Further, as the leader assigns the step to be observed by an individual, the leader can say, "Bob," (who can't read) "I want you to take step three. I will point to three as Mary does it, and I will also look at you so you know when to be particularly listening." Of course, leaders will want to be subtle and provide the same instructions for other observers, even those who can read, so that those with reading difficulties are not singled out.

Intercurrent life events at times made it difficult for group members to attend particular ART sessions. Rather than let attendance and perhaps membership slide, we responded to such occurrences with either "home visit ART" or "phone visit ART." These were visits by one of the group leaders in person or by phone to the absent family. In addition to reassuring the absentee about our interest in their continuing, such visits were used in listening to new or recurring life crisis, and truncated teaching or reteaching of crisis-relevant Structured Learning or Anger Control skills.

It will be important for leaders to note, probably in writing (since remembering from week to week can be difficult), in what specific situation, where, and with whom the parent is agreeing to try the skill at home. We suggest that, if possible, someone from the group follow up with that parent during the week to act as moral support and to help ensure that the skill is tried. Selection of the person might be done by address proximity (to allow for a personal visit especially for those without phones), by volunteer, or by request of the person presently practicing the skill. We suggest that it be made clear that the person doing follow-up not accept "I haven't had a chance to try the skill yet" as a reason for not trying the skill.

GROUP BUILDING

Many families, such as those in our project, are socioeconomically deprived and interpersonally isolated. Belonging to a supportive group may be their first experience in linking in a positive way to the outside world. We entertain no illusions about the place of the ART group initially in the lives of the families. Trust is very low among participants, with ambivalence being the overriding feeling. It is in response to such ambivalence, and the possibility of overcoming it, that activities beyond the group meetings become important. Such activities can build a sense of identity with the group, heighten group cohesiveness, and enhance participation among group members. The following are a few ideas that have been successful for us in achieving these group building goals.

Social gatherings in which food, informal socializing, and possibly other pleasant activities were provided seemed to be a good beginning activity. Such activities for the project group included potluck dinners, holiday parties, bowling parties, birthdays, picnics, and a one-year anniversary dinner. No matter when a group starts, there will probably be a holiday just around the corner that offers an excuse for a party or social get-together. For example, we started in October and held a holiday party just after the first of the year. That particular party consisted of a potluck dinner with fun activities afterwards. Getting a member of the group to head up such a dinner (taking care of signing up who will bring what, etc.) helps take part of the load off the leaders and helps the event become one managed by and for the parents. The leader was usually more than willing and able to get group members to cooperate. We recall several instances of people straggling in at all different times for a dinner whose starting time had been previously announced. Finally, one parent who was tired of having the rest of the group held up, announced, "I'm sick of people being late! Next time, we will eat at 6, whether people are here or not!" From then on, most of the usual latecomers were on time! For the activity after the meal, we suggest ones that don't cost money, and, ideally, ones that call for creativity from the group. One of our most successful after-dinner activities was a game of charades played by both adults and children. On another occasion, each family was invited to bring a game or activity to share. Of course, after summer picnics, swimming, baseball, and other games are logical after-meal activities. You may also have access to community resources and ideas to offer for activities. For example, one of us knew a teenager who was trying to perfect his magic act and was willing to perform for us for free, just for the experience. As a tax-exempt group, you might be able to take advantage of some activities, such as bowling, at a reduced rate. If your agency or project has the money, we suggest that you subsidize such activities to allow everyone to participate.

One of the first things we recommend you do is to purchase an inexpensive camera so that you can take candid photos of the dinners and activities. We found our families to be very enthusiastic and amused as they looked at the pictures again and again. We also found assembling a scrapbook to be an enjoyable way of reliving pleasant times together and reviewing our group history. The scrap book need not be limited to photos, but can also include a written description of the gathering and participants.

After your group has been meeting for a few months, you might want to consider putting a newsletter together. It need not be elaborate; a recapping of group and individual happenings to date is sufficient. Such things as upcoming get-togethers, a review of recent get-togethers, condolences, congratulations, and any personal items an individual wishes to share, such as how the group is relevant for him or her, can be included. You may also want to include items about the children's progress and tell a little about what they have been doing in their group. Children might be invited to share their creativity, as well, such as through poetry or a brief essay.

The following is one of the newsletters we have created.

The Parent Angerbusters Newsletter
Vol. III November 1987

Parents Celebrate First Year Anniversary Party

On Saturday evening, October 24, more than 30 persons, including families, children, relatives, DFY representative, group facilitators and others attended a feast organized by the parents at the home of Rev. Thomas and Mrs. Dorothy Thomas at 19 Gordon St. Those in attendance enjoyed a sumptuous dinner of turkey prepared by Mrs. Mamie Barson, cakes, cold drinks, coffee, tea, fruit. Items were donated by various families, group facilitators, Prof. Goldstein,a nd DFY Representative, Alan Alcon who, in addition to donating a basket of fruit, brought the group DFY Director Leonard Dunston's congratulations to the group and good wishes. Families represented at the function included the Mitchells, the MacArthurs, the Wilsons, the Fernandez, the Irwins, the Burns family, the Greenes, the Harrisons. Professor Arnold Goldstein, A.R.T. Project Director, Ibrahim Rubama, Mary Jane Irwin (Co-facilitator of the group), Mr. Marshall Walker of DFY and Ms. Claudia McCartney of the Youth A.R.T. group also attended. A number of speakers including Messrs. Alcon and Goldstein praised the group and its leadership in this important area of parental involvement and calling them real pioneers.

Letter Inviting Other Parents to Join — by Diane Harrison, Associate Editor and Parent

The reason I joined the group meeting is because I had two kids who had just come home from other placements. And I thought that by joining parents of kids similar to mine, I could talk freely and discuss different ways of dealing with our children. I went and enjoyed the group very much. Because you will see, you are not going through the problems all by yourself. All the parents here have been there. I urge you to join us; learn some skills with us; and I know you will learn a lot and enjoy yourself. Call your YST worker for details at 428-4165 or ask for Ibrahim. We welcome Mrs. Williams to the group, and are happy that Minnie can now join us more regularly with change in her work schedule.

Labor Day Picinic

It was an overcast day but spirits were high for our Labor Day Picnic at Lakeshore Park. Those families attending included the Wilsons, the Harrisons, the Fernandez family, Mary Jane Irwin, and Ibrahim Rubama. The warm but overcast day allowed for foot soccer, building sand castles, Frisbee playing and long walks. As always the food was delicious and there was plenty to go around. It was nice to have Rosemary and Juan with us.

A Note of Thanks

We the Angerbusters wish to thank Mr. Larry DiStefano, Mr. Jim Detore and Mr. Don Klaben for their continued support of our group.

Upcoming Events

Pizza Party

Please plan to attend our Pizza Party, Wednesday December 9, 7–8:30 PM at our regular meeting place at NorthEast Family Center, Hawley Ave. The original party originally planned for November 21 at Mary Fernandez's house at 1405 Butternut St. had to be cancelled due to bad weather. Activities will be planned for the children, and we promise a good time for all.

Holiday Party

January 2nd will be our Holiday Party. We will also be helping Dorothy Greene celebrate her birthday, originally slated for December 19. This party will be held at the home of Rev. and Mrs. Greene, 36 Cannon St. The menu includes ham, scalloped potatoes, zita, and of course birthday cake and ice cream to help Dorothy celebrate her birthday. Bring a small gift (no more than $2) to exchange with another person. Better yet, instead of buying a gift, think about baking cookies, bring a plant, or giving a gift of a special talent you have. Birthday remembrances for Dorothy will also be welcome.

Condolences

Our heartfelt condolences go to Mrs. Mamie Barson, who has experienced a number of tragedies lately. Recently, we learned with sadness the death of her brother. We wish you well and pray you continue to be strong knowing we care.

Congratulations

Youths Margarite, Lena Rose and Connie have been excelling in their school work. We wish them continued success. And special congratulations to Carson also.

Diane Harrison and her children and the Wilsons made big moves to new locations recently. We wish them the best.

Elementary Structured Learning

What the kids have been doing is learning different skills. Some examples are: saying thank you, sharing, knowing your feelings, listening, saying no, dealing with fear, and many others. We also practice "Anger Control" where the kids act out an experience of anger and follow the anger control steps. The kids have really been doing a great job in participating in the group. It would be greatly appreciated if when parents can't make it to the group that they will still send their kids. It's sometimes difficult when the kids aren't at the group because they lose out on learning skills and it's had to catch them up. So please everyone try to make it. We love seeing you. – Leslie and Tracey

Speedy Recovery Prayed For

Mrs. Rosetta had surgery on her eye recently. We all wish her speedy recovery.

Gray Days

Gray Days are when we can't play
And when we can't play, I wish it was May
Gray Days are days I don't like in special ways
So very on the very gray days
On those gray days I'm so bored

I watch TV then pull out the cord
—Connie Burns

Wednesday Meetings

Wednesday we have the meeting
And Leslie always gives me greetings
On Wednesday when we have the meetings and Leslie gives me her
greetings Tracy gives me her looks and her ways and I give her my OK's
—Connie Burns

Newsletters are good to leave with prospective members when you call on them inviting them to join the group.

In this section, we have described the parent meetings, including the three suggested components: (1) review of the week's happenings among group members, (2) presentation and practice of the sessions' skills, and (3) group building activities.

SUMMARY

In this chapter, we have provided information intended to be useful in helping the reader begin and successfully run an Aggression Replacement Training Parents Group. We believe that parents' groups offering Structured Learning of prosocial skills and Anger Control Training are likely to be valuable in themselves. However, to the extent that *all* family members—parents, youth, and younger siblings—can be exposed to the same or complementary interventions (in this case, ART), change toward more healthful behaviors may be enhanced. Likewise, to the extent that the parent group component of ART has positive backing of its sponsoring agency and is a viable part of the youth and sibling ART offerings, its effectiveness is likely to be enhanced

Chapter 5
Program Evaluation

In this chapter, we examine the effectiveness of our Aggression Replacement Training according to a variety of relevant outcome criteria. First we summarize our earlier evaluations of this approach, conducted with incarcerated youth (Goldstein & Glick, 1987). This summary provides a concrete sense of the Aggression Replacement Training curriculum, and the methodology and measures we employ in testing its efficacy. The positive outcome of our initial studies served as strong encouragement in support of our effort to utilize and evaluate the impact of Aggression Replacement Training in a community context.

Our discussion describes our evaluation in full, providing information on design, assessment, program content, and results. It also seeks to give a sense of the difficult and complex research methodology and program implementation issues that emerge in the conduct of community-based delinquency-intervention evaluation

PREVIOUS EVALUATIONS

Our two earlier examinations of the effectiveness of Aggression Replacement Training were both conducted at New York State Division for Youth facilities for adjudicated delinquent males. The first examination included 60 youth, age 14 to 17, convicted of such crimes as assault, burglary, auto theft, possession of stolen property, and drug use. The second examination involved 51 juvenile offenders, age 13 to 21, incarcerated for such crimes as murder, manslaughter, rape, and arson. In each population, the youth were systematically divided into groups receiving (1) Aggression Replacement Training, (2) Brief Instructions (motivation enhancement but no training), or (3) no training. Aggression Replacement Training was conducted for a 10-week period, in the belief that a trial of that length was sufficient to bring about at least beginning discernible changes in participating youth (i.e., changes on outcome criteria large enough to distinguish Training from Brief Instruction or No Training conditions).

The 10-week Aggression Replacement Training curriculum required participating youth to attend three classes each week, one each in Structured Learning, Anger Control, and Moral Reasoning. The content of this curriculum is summarized in Table 5.1.

The results of both evaluations were strongly positive. High levels of Structured Learning skill acquisition were found in both comparisons, as were significant decreases in impulsiveness as rated by facility staff. In one population, the number and intensity of aggressive behavioral incidents declined significantly; in the other population, prosocial alternative behaviors and moral reasoning behaviors both increased significantly. Especially important was our examination of how the short-term positive changes carried over into the community. (We tested the first sample only, since the second group was serving long sentences and very few were released during the study period.) In a study of the youth's functioning in the community four months after they were released, parole personnel doing separate, blind ratings found that youth receiving Aggression Replacement Training significantly exceeded those who did not in rated quality of functioning at home, at work, with peers, and with the community justice system. Thus, the findings of the two evaluation projects combine to indicate that ART is apparently a viable intervention for delinquent youth, substantially reducing aggression and impulsiveness and increasing prosocial behavior, moral reasoning level, and favorable, early postrelease community adjustment. As we noted earlier:

> Although [our assessment] seemed to indicate that young people who participated in ART were able to transfer their learning to situations outside of their institutional environment, we believe that without further intervention such transfer effects will not be sustained . . . the evaluation effort reported here seems to be a valuable beginning effort at constructing a comprehensive intervention for aggressive youths, but it is only a beginning. Many major questions of efficacy remain, especially with relevance to in-community impact. Such questions seem to be well worth addressing. (Goldstein & Glick, 1987)

COMMUNITY-BASED PROJECT

Design

With the facility-based findings as our springboard, we planned and conducted a two-year evaluation of the effectiveness of ART when provided to youth ($N = 84$) on a postrelease, living-in-the-community basis.

Table 5.1. Aggression Replacement Training Curriculum

Week	Structured Learning	Moral Reasoning	Anger Control
1	Expressing a Complaint 1. Define what the problem is, and who's responsible for it. 2. Decide how the problem might be solved. 3. Tell that person what the problem is and how it might be solved. 4. Ask for a response. 5. Show that you understand his or her feelings. 6. Come to agreement on the steps to be taken by each of you.	1. The Used Car 2. Dope Pusher 3. Riots in Public Places	Introduction 1. Rationale: Presentation and discussion 2. Rules: Presentation and discussion 3. Training procedures: Presentation and discussion 4. Contracting for ACT participation 5. Initial history taking regarding antecedent provocations-behavioral response-consequence (A-B-C)
2	Responding to the Feelings of Others (empathy) 1. Observe the other person's words and actions. 2. Decide what the other person might be feeling, and how strong the feelings are. 3. Decide whether it would be helpful to let the other person know you understand his or her feelings. 4. Tell the other person, in a warm and sincere manner, how you think he or she is feeling.	1. The Passenger Ship 2. The Case of Charles Manson 3. LSD	Assessment 1. Hassle Log: Purposes and mechanics 2. Anger self-assessment: physiological cues 3. Anger reducers: Reducer #1. Deep breathing training Reducer #2. Refocusing: Backward counting Reducer #3. Peaceful imagery
3	Preparing for a Stressful Conversation 1. Imagine yourself in the stressful situation. 2. Think about how you will feel and why you will feel that way. 3. Imagine that other person in the stressful situation. Think about how that person will feel and why. 4. Imagine yourself telling the other person what you want to say. 5. Imagine what he or she will say. 6. repeat the above steps using as many approaches as you can think of. 7. Choose the best approach.	1. Shoplifting 2. Booby Trap 3. Plagiarism	Triggers 1. Identification of provoking stimuli (a) Direct triggers (from others) (b) Indirect triggers (from self) 2. Role play: Triggers + cues + anger reducer 3. Review of Hassle Logs

Week	Structured Learning	Moral Reasoning	Anger Control
4	Responding to Anger 1. Listen openly to what the other person has to say. 2. Show that you understand what the other person is feeling. 3. Ask the other person to explain anything you don't understand. 4. Show that you understand why the other person feels angry. 5. If it is appropriate, express your thoughts and feelings about the situation.	1. Toy Revolver 2. Robin Hood Case 3. Drugs	Reminders (Anger Reducer #4) 1. Introduction to self-instruction training 2. Modeling use of reminders under pressure 3. Role play: Triggers + cues + reminders + anger reducer 4. Homework assignments and review of Hassle Log

5	Keeping Out of Fights
	1. Stop and think about why you want to fight.
	2. Decide what you want to happen in the long run.
	3. Think about other ways to handle the situation besides fighting.
	4. Decide on the best way to handle the situation and do it.
		1. Private Country Road
		2. New York vs. Gerald Young
		3. Saving a Life
			Self-Evaluation
			1. Review of reminder homework assignments
			2. Self-evaluation of post-conflict reminders
			    (a) Self-reinforcement techniques
			    (b) Self-coaching techniques
			3. Review of Hassle Log post-conflict reminders
			4. Role play: Triggers + cues + reminders + anger reducer + self-evaluation

6	Helping Others 1. Decide if the other person might need and want your help. 2. Think of the ways you could be helpful. 3. Ask the other person if he/she needs and wants your help. 4. Help the other person.	1. The Kidney Transplant 2. Bomb Shelter 3. Misrepresentation	Thinking Ahead (Anger Reducer #5) 1. Estimating future negative consequences for current acting out 2. Short-term vs. long-term consequences 3. Worst to least consequences 4. Role play: "If. . .then. . ." thinking ahead 5. Role play: Triggers + cues + reminders + anger reducers + self-evaluation + SLT skill
7	Dealing with an Accusation 1. Think about what the other person has accused you of. 2. Think about why the person might have accused you. 3. Think about ways to answer the person's accusations. 4. Choose the best way and do it.	1. Lt. Berg 2. Perjury 3. Doctor's Responsibility	The Angry Behavior Cycle 1. Review of Hassle Logs 2. Identification of own anger-provoking behavior 3. Modification of own anger-provoking behavior 4. Role play: Triggers + cues + reminders + anger reducers + self-evaluation + SLT skill

(continued)

Table 5.1. (*continued*)

Week	Structured Learning	Moral Reasoning	Anger Control
8	Dealing with Group Pressure 1. think about what the other people want you to do and why. 2. Decide what you want to do. 3. Decide how to tell the other people what you want to do. 4. Tell the group what you have decided.	1. Noisy child 2. The Stolen Car 3. Discrimination	Full Sequence Rehearsal 1. Review of Hassle Logs 2. Role play: Triggers + cues + reminders + anger reducers + self-evaluation + SLT skill
	Expressing Affection 1. Decide if you have good feelings about the other person. 2. Decide whether the other person would like to know about your feelings. 3. Decide how you might best express your feelings. 4. choose the right time and place to express your feelings. 5. Express affection in a warm and caring manner.		
9		1. Defense of Other Persons 2. Lying in Order to Help Someone 3. Rockefeller's Suggestion	Full Sequence Rehearsal 1. Review of Hassle Log 2. Role play: Triggers + cues + reminders + anger reducers + self-evaluation + SLT skill
10	Responding to Failure 1. Decide if you have failed. 2. Think about both the personal reasons and the circumstances that have caused you to fail. 3. Decide how you might do things differently if you tried again. 4. Decide if you want to try again. 5. If it is appropriate, try again, using your revised approach.	1. The Desert 2. The Threat 3. Drunken Driving	Full Sequence Rehearsal 1. Review of Hassle Log 2. Role play: Triggers + cues + reminders + anger reducers + self-evaluation + SLT skill

As discussed in chapter 2, we are also aware of the potent contribution to functioning in the community that parents and others may make in the lives of delinquent youth. This belief led to our attempt to discern the effects of offering ART not only to youth, but, for training in reciprocal skills, also to their parents and other family members. Our experimental design is depicted in Table 5.2.

As Table 5.2 depicts, the community-based project is essentially a three-way comparison of ART provided directly to youth (i.e., "community-functioning ART") plus ART provided to youth's parents or other family members (i.e., "community-support ART), versus ART for youth only, versus no-ART control group youth. Largely as a result of how long the New York State Division for Youth has aftercare responsibility for youth discharged from one of their facilities, the ART program offered to project participants was designed to last three months, meeting twice per week, for a planned total of approximately 25 sessions. Each session, one and one-half to two hours long, was spent in (1) brief discussion of current life events and difficulties, (2) Structured Learning skills training (of a skill relevant to the life events/difficulties discussed) and, on an alternating basis, (3) Anger Control Training and Moral Education. The substance of these sessions for youth is presented in chapter 3. Once weekly, an ART session was held for the parents and other family members of a sample of participating youth, as described in chapter 4. Those parents selected to participate, but who did not appear, were provided ART in modified form via a weekly home visit or phone visit.

Assessment

Our goal in designing this community-based project was to examine the effectiveness of ART on both proximal and distal criteria. The former included skills acquisition and anger control; the latter focused on indices of community adjustment and recidivism. Consistent with our interest in family influences on intervention efficacy, we also assessed possible family environment characteristics associated with recidivism. Specific project measures were:

The Skill Checklist (Goldstein, Sprafkin, Gershaw, & Klein, 1979)

Table 5.2. Evaulation Design for ART in the Community

	Trainee Evaluation Condition		
	I	II	III
ART for Delinquent Youths	X	X	—
ART for Parents and Family	X	—	—

consists of brief descriptions of the 50 interpersonal, aggression-management, feelings-related, stress-management or cognitive skills constituting the ART curriculum. The measure's response format permits youth to rate the perceived frequency with which they believe they use each given skill well. The Skill Checklist, in a manner similar to its use in the community project, was employed as a direct measure of perceived skill competence on a pre–post basis in our earlier Aggression Replacement Training studies, the positive outcomes of which may appropriately be viewed as predictive validity evidence speaking in favor of its continued employment for program evaluation purposes.

The Anger Situation Inventory is a 66-item questionnaire developed by Hoshmand, Austin, and Appell (1981; Hoshmand & Austin, 1987) designed to assess both the testee's overall level of self-reported anger arousal, as well as the degree of anger aroused in the individual as a function of several different types of potentially provocative situations.

The Family Environment Scale (Moos & Insel, 1974) is a well-standardized measure of the respondent's perceptions of the nature and quality of the family environment in which they live. Scale subscores are given for cohesion, expressiveness, conflict, independence, achievement orientation, moral-religious emphasis, control, organization, intellectual-cultural, and active-recreational.

Recidivism data were obtained from agency files and interviews with each participant's Youth Service Team caseworker regarding rearrest during the six months following release from facility, our operational measure of recidivism. We are keenly aware of the cautions appropriately associated with this choice of criterion. Farrington, Ohlin, and Wilson (1986) comment in this regard:

> The major dependent variable in most existing experiments is the recidivist/nonrecidivist dichotomy obtained from official records. This is inadequate in many respects. First of all, recidivism has a wide variety of meanings, such as police contacts, arrests, convictions, parole violation, and reimprisonment . . . . Second, the official records reflect the behavior not only of offenders but also of official agencies . . . . it is important to know if a treatment has affected crime or the reaction to crime. Third, the occurrence of one offense during a follow-up period is rather uninformative. In the past, researchers have drawn unduly pessimistic conclusions from high recidivism rates. Even if 90% of persons treated in a particular way are rearrested, this does not necessarily mean that the treatment was ineffective. The treatment might have caused a marked reduction in the frequency or seriousness of offending or in the length of the criminal career. To interpret a recidivist event as a failure implies that complete reformation is likely, whereas all the evidence from self-reported offending studies shows that offending (at least of less serious varieties) is widespread. An implication of this last argument is that more sensitive measures of offending are needed, preferably based on interviews or observation as well as on official records. (p. 37)

Our original measurement intent was to be responsive to both the spirit and substance of this viewpoint and to define recidivism as a multicomponent criterion consisting of rearrest, school or work adjustment, and biweekly ratings completed by a family member of youth behavior in the community. For the many reasons presented in chapters 3 and 4 as the basis for communication difficulties, attendance difficulties and commitment difficulties associated with providing interventions to disadvantaged clients living in often disorganized and stressful life circumstances, obtaining reliable data regarding the youth's school, work, and community adjustment proved impossible – in spite of our energetic efforts to do so. Our choice of rearrest as the project's recidivism criterion was, therefore, our best solution given these data-gathering obstacles.

Results

Interpersonal Skills.   Since the ART groups constituting the project's two treatment conditions, in collaboration with their respective trainers, chose which of the 50 Skillstreaming curriculum skills they wished to learn, different groups learned different, if overlapping, sets of skills. We did not, therefore, examine in our statistical analysis participant change on individual skills. Instead, analysis focused upon total skill change for the ART-participating youth (Conditions 1 and 2) versus non-ART control group youth (Condition 3). The resultant 2 × 3, repeated measures analysis of variance yielded a significant F-value for condition ($F = 7.64$, $df = 2, 83, p < .01$). Post-hoc cell comparisons revealed that both Condition 1 (ART for youth and for family) and Condition 2 (ART for youth only), while not differing significantly from one another, each increased significantly in their overall interpersonal skill competence compared to Condition 3 (no-ART) youth. Table 5.3 lists and defines the 50 skills constituting the training targets of the interpersonal skills component of ART.

Anger Control.   A series of 2 × 3 analyses of variance were conducted on Anger Situation Inventory subscale and total scores (pre- and post-) across the three project conditions. The results of these analyses are presented in Table 5.4. In all instances in which significant Fs are reported, both Condition 1 and Condition 2 are significantly lower in mean anger arousal than Condition 3.

Table 5.5 provides a sample of the Anger Situation Inventory items that define each Inventory subscale.

The pattern of potential anger-arousing situations that do and do not change in their self-reported arousal potency for youths receiving ART versus those who do not is of interest. Table 5.6 summarizes these findings.

Table 5.3. Interpersonal Skills

1. Listening: Do you pay attention to someone who is talking and make an effort to understand what is being said?
2. Starting a Conversation: Do you start conversations with other people and then continue to talk with them for a while?
3. Having a Conversation: Do you talk to other people about things that are interesting to both you and the other person?
4. Asking a Question: Do you think about additional information you need to know and then ask the right person for that information?
5. Saying Thank-You: Do you let other people know that you are thankful they did something for you?
6. Introducing Yourself: Do you make an effort to get to know new people?
7. Introducing Other People: Do you help introduce new people to others?
8. Giving a Compliment: Do you tell other people that you like something about them or what they are doing?
9. Asking for Help: Do you ask for help when you need it?
10. Joining In: Do you figure out the best way to join in with a group that is already involved in an activity, and then join in?
11. Giving Instructions: Do you explain instructions well so that others can follow them easily?
12. Following Instructions: Do you pay careful attention to instructions and then follow them?
13. Apologizing: Do you tell others that you are sorry when you do something that you know is wrong?
14. Convincing Others: Do you try to persuade others that your ideas might be better or more useful than their own?
15. Knowing Your Feelings: Do you try to understand and recognize which emotions you are feeling?
16. Expressing Your Feelings: Do you let others know how you are feeling?
17. Understanding the Feelings of Others: Do you try to figure out what other people are feeling?
18. Dealing with Someone Else's anger: Do you try to understand why the other person is feeling angry?
19. Expressing Affection: Do you let others know that you care about them?
20. Dealing with Fear: When you are feeling afraid, do you try to figure out why, and then try to do something about it?
21. Rewarding Yourself: Do you give yourself a reward after you do something well?
22. Asking Permission: Do you figure out when permission is needed before doing something, and then ask the right person for permission?
23. Sharing Something: Do you offer to share your things with others?
24. Helping Others: Do you give help to others who might need or want assistance?
25. Negotiating: If you and someone else disagree over something, do you try to work out an agreement that will satisfy both of you?
26. Using Self-Control: Do you control your temper so that things do not get out of hand?
27. Standing Up for Your Rights: Do you assert your rights by letting people know where you stand on an issue?
28. Responding to Teasing: Do you remain in control of yourself when others tease you?
29. Avoiding Trouble with Others: Do you stay out of situations that might get you in trouble?
30. Keeping Out of Fights: Do you think of ways other than fighting to handle difficult situations.
31. Making a Complaint: do you tell others in a clear but not angry way when they have done something you don't like?
32. Answering a Complaint: Do you try to listen to other people and answer fairly when they complain about you?

33. Sportmanship After the Game: Do you compliment the other team after a game if they deserve it?
34. Dealing with Embarrassment:Do you do things that help you feel less embarrassed or self-conscious?
35. Dealing with Being Left Out: Do you decide when you have been left out of some activity and then do things to feel better about the situation?
36. Standing Up for a Friend: Do you let others know when you feel that a friend has not been treated fairly?
37. Responding to Persuasion: If another person is trying to convince you of something, do you think about what the other person believes, and then what you believe, before deciding what to do?
38. Responding to Failure: Do you try to figure out the reason for failing in a particular situation, and then decide what you can do in order to be more successful in the future?
39. Dealing with Contradictory Messages: Do you recognize and deal with the confusion that results when others tell you one thing but say or do something else?
40. Dealing with an Accusation: Do you figure out what you have been accused of and why, and then decide on the best way to deal with the person who made the accusation?
41. Getting Ready for a Difficult Conversation: Do you try to figure out what you and another person might say *before* you have a stressful conversation with that other person?
42. Dealing with Group Pressure: Do you decide what *you* want to do when others want you to do something else?
43. Deciding on Something to Do: If you are feeling bored, do you try to find something interesting to do?
44. Deciding What Caused a Problem: If a problem comes up, do you try to figure out what caused it?
45. Seeing a Goal: Do you realistically decide on what you would like to accomplish before starting a task?
46. Deciding on Your Abilities: Do you try to realistically figure out how well you might do at a particular task before you start it?
47. Gathering Information: Do you decide what you need to know and how to get that information?
48. Arranging Problems by Importance: Do you decide realistically which of your problems is most important and should be dealt with first?
49. Making a Decision: Do you consider different possibilities and then choose the one which you feel will be best?
50. Concentrating on a Task: Are you able to ignore distractions and pay attention to what you want to do?

The two arrays of potential anger-arousing stimulus situations presented in Table 5.6 seem clearly distinguishable to us in their "stimulus-pull" or inherent provocation potential. ART has shown to have the capacity to somewhat defuse the less potent situations. Physical abuse, control, or coercion from others, having one's personal space invaded, and betrayal of trust each intuitively seems to us to be inherently strong provocations, the response to which, it appears, was not moderated by ART participation.

Family Environment. The results we have reported for interpersonal skills and anger arousal control are hypothesis-testing findings. We pre-

Table 5.4. Analyses of Variance for Anger Situation Inventory Scores

Situation	*F*	*P*
Seeing Others Abused	4.93	.001
Intrusion	1.74	ns
Personal Devaluation	6.49	.001
Betrayal of Trust	2.41	ns
Minor Nuisance	7.79	.001
Control/Coercion	1.20	ns
Verbal Abuse	7.28	.001
Physical Abuse	2.41	ns
Unfair Treatment	4.52	.001
Goal Blocking	7.48	.001
Neutral	.73	ns
Total	6.47	.001

dicted and found substantial between-condition differences favoring ART participation in these two dependent variable domains. Our interest in the family environment, the domain to which we now turn, was more exploratory in nature. Consistent with the systems view that underlies the present project in general, and its family and siblings groups in particular, we wished to inquire broadly into the relevance of the family environment—as perceived by the delinquent youths—for our project's "bottom line" dependent variable—recidivism. We sought to explore the degree to which youth who subsequently are and are not rearrested differ in their perceptions of their family environment upon their release from incarceration and return to in-community living. Table 5.7 presents these comparative perceptions.

In an attempt to identify family environment predictors of later recidivsm, *t*-tests were conducted comparing mean scores for recidivists versus nonrecidivists on each family environment score (FES) subscale. None of the comparisons thus conducted reached acceptable levels of statistical significance. As Druckman (1979) had found in an earlier investigation, these findings fail to support the utility of perceived family environment as a predictor of subsequent youth recidivism.

Recidivism.   The large majority of previously incarcerated youth who recidivate do so within the first six months after release (Maltz, 1984). Thus, rearrest, the recidivism criterion employed in the current project, was tracked for that time period. For Condition 1 and Condition 2 youth, the six-month tracking period consisted of the first three months during which they received ART and three subsequent no-ART months. Condition 3 youth, of course, received no ART during the entire tracking period. Chi-square analysis examining the frequency of rearrest by condition showed a significant effect for ART participation. As reflected in

Table 5.5. Sample Subscale Items from the Anger Situation Inventory

---

Seeing Others Abused
    Seeing a friend being put ddown.
    You see someone attacked by a group.
    You see a parent slap a small child's face
Intrusion
    Someone talks loudly right behind you in a movie
    Someone uses your belongings without asking.
    Someone walks into your place without asking.
Personal Devaluation
    Being told by your employer that you have done poor work.
    Being teased or laughed at.
    Somebody calls you a liar.
Betrayal of Trust
    Finding out that a friend has talked about you behind your back.
    Somebody you trust cheats you or rips you off.
    Somebody you trust breaks an important promise to you.
Minor Nuisance
    Being overcharge or short-changed.
    Somebody repeatedly asking to borrow things from you.
    Someone playing the radio real loud.
Control/coercion
    Someone orders you to do as he says.
    Being told to do something you don't want to do.
    Someone takes away your privileges.
Verbal Abuse
    Being shouted at.
    Someone swears at you with foul language.
    Somebody talks to you in a threatening tone of voice.
Physical Abuse
    Someone throws something at you.
    Being pushed or shoved by someone in an argument.
    Someone slaps your face.
Unfair Treatment
    Being punished more than you deserve.
    Others get served before you, out of turn.
    Somebody accuses you of something you have not done.
Goal Blocking
    Somebody refuses to tell you something you really need to know.
    Not getting a job you apply for.
    Being refused admission to a place you want to be in.
Neutral
    Someone invites you to a party.
    Somebody pay you a compliment.
    Sombody does you a favor.

Table 5.8, both Condition 1 and Condition 2 youth were rearrested significantly less often than were youth not receiving ART ($X^2 = 8.25$, $df = 2$, $p < .02$).

An additional aspect of these recidivsm data is of interest. The 39 youth who received ART only may be partitioned into two subsamples reflecting the degree of the intensity of community supervision provided to

Table 5.6. ART Change versus No-ART Change on
Anger Situation Inventory Scales

Significant ART vs. No-ART Differences	No Significant ART vs No-ART Differences
Seeing Others Abused	Intrusion
Personal Devaluation	Betrayal of Trust
Minor Nuisance	Control/Coercion
Verbal Abuse	Physical Abuse
Unfair Treatment	Neutral
Goal Blocking	
Total	

Table 5.7. Mean Family Environment Scores for Recidivists and Nonrecidivists

FES Scale	Recidivists	Nonrecidivists
Cohesion	45.06	42.48
Expressiveness	43.56	42.71
Conflict	51.19	56.17
Independence	46.87	42.75
Achievement	52.13	51.42
Intellectual/Cultural	38.68	42.65
Active/Recreational	50.37	50.54
Moral/Religious	46.00	49.02
Organization	50.30	51.20
Control	51.18	56.17

Table 5.8. Frequency of Rearrest by Condition

Condition	Total N	Rearrested N	Rearrested %
Youth ART + Parent/Sibling ART	13	2	15
Youth ART Only	39	6	15
No ART Control	32	14	43

them. A hypothetical dimension of degree of supervision, from most to least, can be depicted as: (1) in facility, (2) in group home, (3) in own home, and (4) no supervision. Eliminating from the recidivism analysis (i.e., analysis of frequency of rearrest while residing in the community) the 19 youth residing in group homes, on the basis that their degree of supervision places them more on an in-facility basis than an in-community basis, one obtains a noteworthy trend in the recidivism pattern of the 65 project youth, all of whom resided in their family's home, as depicted in Table 5.9.

While the result of the chi-square analysis of these data is not statistically significant ($X^2 = 3.51$, $df = 2$, $p > .05$), a trend is evident suggesting the possible value of broader, more sustained ART involve-

Table 5.9. Frequency of Rearrest with Group Home Youth Eliminated

Condition	Total N	Rearrested N	Rearrested %
Youth ART + Parent/Sibling ART	13	2	15
Youth ART Only	20	6	30
No ART Control	32	14	43

ment of in-community figures who are significant in the lives of delinquent youth, including parents, siblings, peers, classmates, employers, and others. We will describe the possible nature of such "total immersion" community involvement in chapter 7.

SUMMARY

As characterized by the outcome of our earlier evaluations of ART when employed with incarcerated youth, its use with juvenile delinquents released into the community provides a pattern of consistent and encouraging results. Self-reported interpersonal skill level improves; anger control increases, at least in response to nonsevere provocations; and recidivism defined in terms of rearrest during the first six months following release diminishes substantially. Beyond these important outcomes, ART provided to youth's parents and siblings appears to augment its efficacy, thus providing implied support for a systems view of delinquency intervention. The expanded use of ART with delinquent youth is strongly encouraged by these findings, as is further inquiry into means for augmenting the potency of efforts to involve and intervene constructively with significant others in the delinquent youth's community environment.

Chapter 6

Administration of Community-Based Programs

Community-based programs for delinquent youth have a reasonable chance for success only when two types of practitioners do their jobs well: the staff who implements the program and the administrator who must manage it. Preceding chapters have addressed primarily the former. We now speak to the administrators and their role in the optimal management of community-intervention programs for youngsters in trouble.

The administration of human services programs, especially those for youth, presents a difficult challenge for the public administrator. Youth programs are usually targeted to meet specific needs and often originate as a result of government funds or private grant awards. Thus, youth programming is often reactive to the state of the economy, and financial support for such programs is often given at the whim of lawmakers. Beyond the financial uncertainties, youth program administrators are faced with a clientele that has minimal political or lobbying influence, since they do not vote and have little or no formal organization.

How, then, does a public administrator optimally manage a youth services system? What policies need to be articulated, how are funds allocated, how are programs delivered within local communities, and what mechanisms for accountability can be instituted? Ultimately, the extent to which a youth program is successful in a community is the extent to which that program becomes a service provided to the community by the community.

HISTORICAL DEVELOPMENT

The organization and administration of youth services programs, whether for general youth development or delinquency prevention, occur by and large at the state or provincial levels of government in North America. Most youth services systems are organized so that the functions of budget planning, fiscal control, program initiatives, personnel, quality assurance, monitoring, and program evaluation occur within a government agency that is charged with the responsibility to set standards, develop regulations, direct policy, and implement the good of the public.

The system of public youth services evolved from a variety of church and child welfare organizations primarily interested in youth who were destitute or in trouble with their communities. As early as 1825, there was a growing concern with the undisciplined behaviors of boys, especially those who were neglected by their families (Empey, 1978). In 1877, the Charity Organization of the Poor and other church-affiliated groups began to support refuge houses and large institutions to care for those children who were without family support or who were deemed troublemakers in their communities. At about the same time, the Society for the Prevention of Pauperism established a house of refuge for such youth in New York City, an intervention approach that was subsequently replicated in several large urban areas of the country. In 1899, the first juvenile court was established in Chicago and was empowered to decide the welfare and future of children, including sending them to institutions to control their delinquent behavior. In the early twentieth century, a more comprehensive youth services system was developed in the United States, including a social services system of child care institutions, as well as a training school system to deal with delinquents incapable of living in their home communities (Empey, 1978).

In spite of this broad development of institutional resources, and perhaps in part because of it, communities in this era typically did little to care for youth and their problems—whether social welfare or delinquency—within their own environs. By 1940, many youth advocacy groups, including the American Law Institute, highlighted the failures of such juvenile institutions. As a consequence of such exposure and concern, a strong movement emerged to establish youth authorities throughout the United States. These authorities were to be responsible for considering the special needs of youth within their jurisdiction and ordering appropriate services for them. Their services ranged from institutional placement to services within the youth's community. The first youth authorities were established in California, Massachusetts, Minnesota, Texas, and Wisconsin. By 1945, states such as New York had formalized their youth commissions into state agencies with the responsibility for developing systems of youth services and programs. But how were these responsibilities to be optimally discharged? How might such agencies be most effectively managed?

MANAGEMENT THEORIES

As we have noted elsewhere (Glick, 1986), administrative responsibilities may be approached from rather diverse, alternative management perspectives. Three clusters of management theories have been identified: chain of command, parent-child management, and developmental-community (Likert, 1967; Bower, 1976).

Public administrators who endorse *chain-of-command* theories structure their organizations in a hierarchical manner. Formal authority, as well as communications, flow from the top of the organization to the bottom. Decision making is done by individuals at or near the top of the organization, whereas decisions are implemented by those near or at the bottom. While an advantage of this organizational structure is the ability to make decisions quickly and with minimal consultation and collaboration, the system requires personnel to spend a great deal of time and effort exercising control over those below them in the hierarchical structure.

The *parent-child-management* theories are those in which the chief executive officer of the system is perceived and behaves as the parent, while the staff are perceived and behave as the children within the system. The struggle between the chief administrator as the parent with the staff as children is central to the growth and development of the system as well as the programs and services within it. The administrator of this type of organization emphasizes human interactions rather than organizational functions, and interactive processes rather than tasks and products.

The *developmental-community management* theories assume social interaction as an integral part of the organization and promote the creation of an environment that supports personal and professional growth. The theories clustered within this area assume that all participants in the organization have the potential for growth and development. Each is presumed to be a multifaceted individual whose various attributes have important implication for the organization. There is held to be a direct positive relationship between the level at which the individual within the organization feels protected, emotionally supported, recognized, and valued, and the individual's ability to function as part of an integrated social group that increases the competence of the structure to plan, solve problems, make decisions, and implement policy. The organizational structure for the theories within the developmental-community area then becomes a human support system capable of responding to the individuals within it in order to meet their personal and professional needs for growth and development. The system also serves to accomplish the mission, goals, and objectives of the organization.

A comparison of generic management issues as reflected in each of the three administrative orientations appears in Table 6.1. The purpose of this comparison is to clarify the philosophical similarities and differences among the three orientations, and to provide a rationale in support of our preference for the developmental-community managerial style. The principles reflected in Table 6.1 illustrate the applicability of these models not only to large complex systems, but also to small, unidimensional direct-services agencies. With this latter focus in mind, we direct our attention to the roles and functions government plays in managing youth services within local communities.

MANAGING COMMUNITY-BASED PROGRAMMING

Even though most youth services systems are organized at the state levels of government, the majority are implemented at local levels by community-based, not-for-profit organizations. Several factors make the delivery of quality youth services difficult to administer effectively, especially while also ensuring cost efficiency. These factors include (1) the establishment of a planning process that involves all interested parties ensuring that appropriate services and programs are available; (2) the development of policies, rules, and regulations that protect the public interest yet allow for municipal home rule; (3) the appropriation of funds in an equitable manner so that all localities and citizens have fair and equal access to services; and (4) the development of a structure for accountability that allows system refinement, program improvement, and fiscal responsibility. Successful public administrators, whether managing statewide systems or community-based operations, will often have a well-articulated theory of management supported by a sound philosophical foundation.

> While most administrators do have an implicit, often vague, philosophical framework from which they operate, rarely do administrators take the opportunity to fully think through their operating philosophy or develop a written philosophical statement of youth programming. Even if a philosophy is developed, it is rarely the product of dialogue among the program's policy managers. The administrator's statement of philosophy must be more than just a series of general goals and ethical statements. Optimally, it is a concrete, detailed, written discourse that includes the following topical areas: the nature of youth and the general characteristics of the targeted population served; the nature of staff and expected standards for staff behavior; a detailed description of the nature of the interactions required between youth and staff as well as staff and staff; and an overview of treatment. (Goldstein & Glick, 1987, p. 248)

Public administrators who manage community-based programs will ideally also address a number of additional concerns:

Table 6.1. A Comparison of Management Issues Across Administrative Orientation

Management Issues	Chain of Command	Parent/Child	Developmental/Community
Organizational (authority) Structure (power)	Hierarchical Pyramid	Hierarchical Vertical	Horizontal Interactional
Problem identification	Department/Unit head	Chief executive officer	All Decision Center/Support groups
Problem resolution	Staff within Department/Unit	Workers in the agency	Decision centers/Support groups determined by delegated roles/functions
Focus of control	External to Staff; external to organizational structure	External to Staff; internal to organizational structure	Internal to staff; internal to organizational structure
Task performance	Assigned to different departments; staff work within work/day, work/week parameters	Workers assume task and complete as required both on and off the job	Assignments divided and monitored by each decision center
Delegated authority	Department/head Unit/head	Chief executive officer	Decision center manager/support group facilitator
Supervisor subordinate line of authority	Staff subordinate to superior	Supervisor limited by staff autonomy	Supervisor retains sphere of influence through decision centers
Decision making authority	Agency/institutional policies	Permission delegated to underlings	Functional within each decision center

Youth Participation

Successful youth programming most likely depends upon the degree to which youth themselves are involved with and participate in the development of their own services and programs. Youth participation means youth empowerment in that administrators must be able and willing to involve youth in the policy and decision-making processes established at every level of organizational structure. This translates into youth representation on agency boards of directors, involvement with budget preparation, resource allocation, as well as policy development. The only limitation is the amount of time and energy available to the youth.

Community Involvement

The public administrator must also grapple with the issues of local autonomy and local initiative. A comprehensive youth services system is more apt to be established if state or higher-level administrators are able to delegate to local communities the capacity to develop programs for themselves. The degree to which communities have a major role in planning their own youth services is, to a large extent, the degree to which such programming will be differentiated, prescriptive, focused, relevant, effective, and cost efficient.

Networking

Public administrators need to develop networks and structures that enhance sound interagency coordination. Basic to this philosophical tenet are efficient fiscal practices. Certainly it seems reasonable to believe that, with interagency coordination, cooperative funding sources, multiple funding cycles, and standardized fiscal practices will develop. Interagency coordination also provides the foundations upon which an array of youth services may be developed, planning may occur, and administration may be implemented. Thus, the interagency coordination effort becomes the cornerstone upon which public administrators may begin to implement reasonable policy for youth services.

Roles and Responsibilities

Public administrators, whether at federal, state, or municipal levels of government, have generic roles and responsibilities to ensure that quality youth services are provided within their jurisdictions. While the specific tasks associated with each role may depend on the public administrator's scope of responsibility, the basic functions of these roles are common to all public administrators. Thus, the ability of the administrator to master each of the roles described below and incorporate them into his or her daily interactions with others, as well as use each as guides in the management of systems, will contribute importantly to the extent to which the public administrator is successful in implementing policies, mandates, and quality youth services.

Advocator.   The public administrator is in a position to set the standards, develop regulations and rules for program operations, and direct monitoring and accountability systems. Within this context, the public administrator must advocate for programs and ensure that they all meet those standards developed. Beyond that, the administrator needs to ensure that advocacy is provided at all levels of government as well as within the private sector so that the youth services necessary may be developed given the availability of resources and systems constraints. Advocacy here means that the public administrator is both willing and able to administer the public good in a fair and equitable manner that is constant and consistent

Coordinator.   The youth services system requires a great deal of coordination. Specifically, it is important that fiscal resources, program development, delivery of service, and inter- and intra-agency communication be coordinated so as to ensure efficient and effective youth services. Therefore, it is important that the public administrator develop a role as coordinator within his or her jurisdiction.

Enabler.   Youth services systems require administrators who are able to facilitate such processes as program application, acquisition of fiscal resources, management of existing programs, or problem solving. The public administrator must develop the role of enabler and be willing to facilitate service providers in the delivery of quality youth programs. Specifically this may include providing technical assistance (e.g., training manuals, guidebooks), as well as interpreting statutes, rules, regulations, and policies.

Planner.   The public administrator is the catalyst for youth services planning. In this role, the administrator must be in a position to stimulate innovation, assist in providing data, analyze trends, direct service-delivery systems in problem identification and resolution, and focus efforts for sound program development. The public administrator in this role must be proactive in developing the delivery system and must be willing to take time in its evolution.

Resourcer.   In this role, the public administrator is responsible for the acquisition, distribution, and management of resources, whether they are fiscal, human, or material. Tasks included in this role are the development of budgets for fiscal appropriation and allocation, the management of fiscal appropriations, and provision of guidelines for resource development and management, and the ability to provide direction and consultation.

STATE MODELS

Effective management of youth services systems must also be attentive to the tensions that naturally exist between that which must be administered systemwide, that which may be relegated to local communities, that which is implemented directly by the public sector, and that which may be contracted privately. In this section, we provide examples of these policy dilemmas in order to highlight the development of community-based programming that is state administered.

Deinstitutionalization

During the early 1970s, national attention turned to the developmentally disabled and to institutionalized populations housed in mental hospitals and centers for the mentally retarded. Many social activists lobbied for community-based programs, and specific cases were identified that illustrated the abuses of large institutions warehousing humans. Administrators of institutions such as the Willowbrook Center for the Mentally Retarded and the Massachusetts Hospital for the Insane were ultimately brought to court, and this action led to decrees for deinstitutionalization. Simultaneously, the special-education movement took on national prominence as educators advocated for educational settings for children with handicapping conditions to be placed in the least restrictive environments for their positive growth and development. These developments, along with the enactment of a tax ceiling act that forced state government to cut institutional youth services and find appropriate alternatives, provided the Commonwealth of Massachusetts the necessary impetus to take action. Thus, in 1972, with the appointment of the first Commissioner of Youth Services, Massachusetts closed its large state institution that served delinquent, aggressive youth. In its stead, the state embarked on what was then considered an innovative public program change.

Community-Based Programming

With the large Massachusetts institutions closed, a gap in services was created for those youngsters traditionally removed from their homes and communities and placed in juvenile delinquency centers. The state developed a system of contracting with private providers in order to ensure juvenile justice services for youth in their local communities. Under the aegis of the second Commissioner of Youth Services, the deinstitutionalization of violent and assaultive youth continued. The number of small, community-based, private facilities initiated under the first appointed commissioner grew. Massachusetts has continued this intervention strategy and now has in place a fully developed system of community-based, secure facilities for the treatment of young juvenile felons.

National Adoption of Community-Based Programming

Other states have developed community-based programs and youth services. In each of the following examples, states were faced with the social policy requirement of establishing deinstitutionalization and least restrictive environments for youth, as well as the fiscal realities of no increase, or in some cases, decreases in revenues.

Through the California Youth Authority, California developed a community development project in which youth were classified and placed according to Interpersonal Levels of Maturity (Warren, 1966). Through this program strategy, California hoped to accomplish meeting the pressures of deinstitutionalization as well as providing a rational approach to placing youngsters in least restrictive environments according to a needs-based classification system.

Texas developed a community-based youth services and detention model. This program strategy was partly a result of the need to manage a large geographical area in a more cost-efficient manner, and partly a result of programmatic differences that existed in different regions. Georgia has developed a community-based intensive supervision and parole model as an alternative to youth incarceration, in response to the growing costs of institutionalizing juveniles, as well as community pressures to deal with high recidivism rates after youth are released.

Although each of these states illustrates examples of community-based youth services delivery systems, only one state—New York—has been able to provide community-based delinquency prevention services within a system that is publically administered yet privately implemented. We believe that the New York State youth services system is unique for a variety of reasons and serves as a model for study and replication. The following is not the only strategy for youth programming; but it is one that has done a good job of addressing the administration and organization of systemwide issues in a well-populated area with complex demographics. The strategies developed take into account such management dilemmas as public versus private implementation of youth services; systemwide accountability; levels of administration (i.e., statewide, countywide, municipal); planning processes that ensure needs identification; and the development of services, program effectiveness, and cost efficiency.

NEW YORK STATE DIVISION FOR YOUTH

The Division for Youth is a state agency that is part of the executive branch of New York state government. The division is one of the few state agencies nationally that is responsible for a juvenile justice system that includes both a mandate for delinquency *prevention* as well as the administration of facilities for juvenile delinquents. While there are both advantages and disadvantages to a unitized juvenile agency, one factor that enhances the public administration of innovative youth services is the ability of a unitized agency to deal with delinquency prevention, rehabilitation, and youth development within its jurisdiction. The Division's mission is *delinquency prevention through positive youth development*. In essence, it is this mission that drives program development, service delivery, and public administration of programs and services.

Public Support and Commitment

New York state has a long and strong involvement with human services, especially youth programs. This commitment is articulated in a variety of ways, including a legislative mandate to the Division for Youth to promote the emotional, social, moral, and physical well-being of youth (persons under 21 years of age) throughout the state. Beyond its stated mission, mandate, and policy, New York has also generously financed youth programming since the inception of the Youth Commission in 1945. New York state budgets as much money for youth development and delinquency prevention for its counties and municipalities as does its federal counterpart (the Office of Juvenile Justice and Delinquency Prevention) budgets for all 50 states.

Youth Development and Delinquency Prevention Funds.   Publically administered, community-based youth programming began with legislation in 1974. As a result of the Youth Development and Delinquency Prevention Act, New York state committed funds to recreational and youth development services in a rational and systematic manner based upon youth population according to the federal census. Each municipality was entitled to a per capita amount of $5.50 per youth per year to develop programs and services within local communities. The state funds were appropriated on a 50% matching formula basis, meaning that each municipality would be reimbursed for up to 50% of what they actually spent for youth programs, to a maximum of their per capita formula. The state legislature, in that same legislation and in support of an existing county government structure, required each county to establish a County Youth Bureau, operated by a lay citizen board, whose director was accountable only to the chief executive officer of the county (i.e., County Manager, Chairperson of the County Board of Supervisors or Legislature, County Executive). Thus, the state of New York supported local governance and autonomy and home rule, and initiated a joint state-county partnership in administering and managing a youth services system for the state. In support of the Youth Bureau structure, the state provided the 50% reimbursement to counties and up to $75,000 per year for administrative costs to operate the Youth Bureau. In 1976, the legislation was amended and enhanced to allow an additional $25,000 to established youth bureaus (county or municipal) for administration, if they had demonstrated that they had spent all of their Youth Development and Delinquency Prevention fund eligibility for the previous two years of operation.

New York state also established, in the 1974 legislation, a planning process by which local communities could draw down state funding for youth services. The establishment of *county comprehensive planning* required the Division for Youth to develop rules and regulations to administer the state financial assistance to counties. Within this fiscal appropriation, New York state provides approximately $41.5 million each year for general youth services programs. These programs fall into 10 broad service areas:

1.   Recreation/Leisure Time. This category of programming is aimed at the general youth population, and its purpose is positive youth development. Programs that enhance the youth's positive self-concept, improve physical and mental growth, and provide opportunities for

achievement, peer relationships, and teamwork are the types that are funded. Examples of such programs are community recreation and youth centers, day camps, summer camps, swim programs, performing arts, and arts and crafts.

2. Community Service/Youth Participation. This category of programming, also aimed at the general youth population, may also be designed for those youth who are potentially the concern of the juvenile justice system or child welfare systems. Objectives for these programs often include individual skill development, community enhancement or beautification, and victim restitution. Thus, program options developed by the public administrator are service-learning projects, youth councils, literacy volunteer programs, neighborhood conservation corps projects, youth as tutors, teacher aides, child care aids activities, or programs that incorporate youth as interns or apprentices.

3. Education. This category of programming is directed primarily at youth with handicapping conditions. These youth, often described as special-needs children, are labeled as emotionally disturbed, learning disabled, or school dropouts. Thus, program options developed and funded for this youth population often include remedial education activities, tutorials, alternative schools, general equivalency diploma programs, institutional field trips, or cultural enlighment or enhancement programs.

4. Employment. This category of programming is also directed at youth who are in the general youth population or are youth at high risk. The high-risk youth are those who may be vulnerable to dependency on public programs or those who return from institutional placement. Some program options include job readiness training, work experience programs, job placement services, job development programs, and apprenticeships.

5. Family Services. This category of youth programming is usually targeted to youth populations that present specific problems, such as children of single parents, latchkey children, or children of teen parents. Thus the public administrator would be interested in funding programs such as family counseling, parenting education, self-help and family support groups, big brother/big sister projects, and school-age child and child care programs.

6. Physical Health. Programs funded in this category are targeted at the general youth population, with special emphasis on sexually active teens, poor families, teen parents, and the physically handicapped. Programs funded in this category usually include first aid instruction, nutrition education, family planning services, sex education, physical rehabilitation, and general health information services.

7. Social/Emotional Adjustment. Youth targeted in this funding cat-

egory are usually those who have specific problems with life situations such as alcoholism, drug abuse, and sexual or physical abuse. Programs usually focus on counseling as an intervention and assist youth with coping mechanisms for a particular problem. These programs include such activities as crisis intervention, psychological testing and evaluation, and outreach services.

8.   Basic Personal Necessities. Those youth who are runaway, homeless, destitute, or victims of family violence are examples of those populations served by this category of programming. Funds are available for programs to provide basic human needs such as food, clothing, shelter, financial assistance, emergency shelters, foster homes, group homes, or independent-living support services.

9.   Legal Services. These programs are available to the general youth population and provide such services as family court advocacy, legal aid, crime victim representation, court monitoring, youth rights training, and other types of advocacy.

10.   Juvenile Justice Services. This category is specifically aimed at youth at risk of becoming involved in the juvenile justice system, or those already in it. Such programs as peer courts, juvenile aid bureaus, court diversion services, and alternative to incarceration projects are examples eligible for funding

Special Delinquency Prevention Program Funds.   While the Youth Development and Delinquency Prevention funds are used to provide resources for the general youth population, the New York state legislature was sensitive to the special needs associated with the causes of juvenile delinquency. Thus, in 1976, an annual appropriation was targeted to delinquency-prevention programs, with special emphasis on those economic, social, and geopolitical factors that cause youth to develop antisocial behaviors.

These funds are administered at the state level in direct contracts with community-based, not-for-profit organizations or by county youth bureaus, with funds allocated directly to them by the state. Programs are reimbursed at 100% levels for projects developed in compliance with the County Comprehensive Plan and that meet one or more of 15 specific targeted groups of youth under 21 years of age who are

- at risk of becoming Persons in Need of Supervision (PINS) or Juvenile Delinquents (JDs), or youth who are charged with committing a crime;
- considered for placement outside the home;
- discharged into the community from institutional care or on parole;

- presently receiving community-based residential care as PINS, JDs, or placed with the Social Services System;
- on probation;
- homeless youth or youth who have run away from home;
- chronically truant or illegally absent from school;
- school dropouts;
- parents or about to become parents, or are children of a teenage parent, and lack adequate family support;
- victims of child abuse, domestic violence, maltreatment, or neglect;
- members of a family that has had frequent involvement in the justice or human services systems or that lacks adequate family support;
- of limited English speaking abilities;
- in critical need of employment support services and jobs;
- involved in prostitution;
- exhibiting self-destructive behaviors.

New York state recognized that some delinquency results from conditions of poverty, and so a portion of these funds are targeted for relevant programs in larger urban areas such as New York City and Buffalo. The remainder of the funds, which approached $14 million during fiscal year 1987, are appropriated by a combination of youth census and a Division of Criminal Justice formula that assigns a juvenile delinquency risk factor to municipalities throughout the state. Once funds are allocated, the Division for Youth is responsible for their administration and for ensuring that contracts are implemented and services are provided as stipulated. Thus, a system of contract monitoring and program evaluation is conducted annually by the state. Additionally, the program ensures that a system of youth services is available at the local community level, provided by grass roots community-based organizations; and that municipal needs are met as identified in a planning process known as County Comprehensive Planning.

The Runaway and Homeless Youth Program.   The state of New York, as part of its mandate to prevent delinquency through positive youth development, provides approximately $6 million to Counties for Runaway and Homeless Youth programming. Initiated in 1977, the runaway programs were developed to provide crisis shelters and counseling programs to people under the age of 18. The purpose of the program is to reunite youngsters with their families and prevent them from entering either the social services systems or the juvenile justice system.

Recognizing that there were also older homeless youth who either had no families to which they could return, or whose families were unwilling to have them return, the state of New York enacted legislation in 1985 that provided for transitional living programs for youth over the age of 16. These programs are certified by the Division for Youth to provide housing for up to one year in addition to brokering employment, training, or educational services for each homeless youth.

Counties are reimbursed for up to 60% of the funds they expend for these programs. They may request to operate runaway and homeless programs once they have developed a runaway and homeless plan, using the same County Comprehensive Planning system. The only restriction is that counties must first identify and provide programs for their runaway population (younger, crisis-intervention services) before they may request funds for their homeless (older, transitional-living) population.

Special Initiatives.   Beyond these funding sources, the public commitment to community-based youth services is also demonstrated by special fiscal appropriations based on identified needs. Currently, monies have been provided by the state legislature to the Division for Youth to operate a job development program in which youngsters who return from institutions to their communities are provided with support services to help them be more economically self-sufficient. These services include such activities as developing employability skills, increasing basic academic skills, as well as locating supervised work situations. Additionally, the Division is also given a special appropriation to contract with counties for Community Care programs and develop models for aftercare services for youth who return to their communities from Division for Youth facilities. The purpose of this program is to ensure that youth are successfully transitioned into their home communities and reduce recidivism.

Thus far, we have described the various funding sources available to the Division for Youth that enable localities to develop a variety of youth programs and services. Summarized in Table 6.2 is the State Aid to Localities administered through the division by type, dollar amount, and fund purpose, for fiscal year 1987.

County Comprehensive Planning

The foundation upon which the New York state youth services system is built is County Comprehensive Planning. The purpose of this process is to

- identify local youth needs and develop effective and efficient strategies to meet those needs;
- convene the appropriate segments of the local community in one planning forum;

Table 6.2. New York State Division for Youth
1987–88 State Aid

Type	Dollar Amount	Purpose
Youth Bureau Admin.	County: $100,000 Municipality: $75,000	To plan, coordinate and allocate resources to meet local youth needs
Youth Dev. Delinq. Prev. (YDDP)	$41.500 million	To fund: (1) youth development services; (2) recreation/leisure time services; and (3) delinquency prevention services
Spec. Delinq. Prevention (SDPP)	$14.550 million[1]	To fund: services for youth at risk of unnecessary or further involvement with the juvenile justice system
Residential Services*	$4.790 million	
*Runaway	$2.570 million	To fund crisis counseling services and emergency shelters for runaway and homeless youth up to 18 years old
*Homeless	$2.220 million	To support the establishment and/ or operation of young adult shelters for 16-21 year olds
TOTAL	$60.820 million	

[1]Includes Insurance, Bonding, Auditing Funds

- coordinate the existing local private and public youth services and programs;
- provide a rational process by which financial resources are allocated and programs funded with state monies;
- empower local communities to administer and implement a youth development and delinquency-prevention services system;
- develop joint responsibility for youth planning and resource allocation given established state policy and public intent.

The planning process requires that the county be responsible to include and involve all those interested in the development of youth programs and services. It relies on the expertise in the local community to provide the input and produce a viable youth services plan. It also presumes that the management of the youth services plan will be coordinated by a local structure, the youth bureau, which is willing and able to administer the public good.

The Division for Youth, through regulation, has defined the components of the Comprehensive Plan and requires each county to include four discrete sections: needs assessment; design of action strategies; implementation; and monitoring/evaluation. The Comprehensive Plan ideally reflects the combined thoughts of all the local youth services providers, administrators, youth, and citizens, and, once approved by the Division, serves as a working document for the development and funding of local youth programs. The following is a detailed description of each section.

Needs Assessment.   The foundation of the comprehensive plan is the needs assessment component. It is designed to provide youth services planners with a logical and systematic method to identify the unmet youth services needs that exist within their communities. This task is accomplished through activities that include data collection, data analysis, and statement of needs. A comparison of youth needs in contrast with existing youth programs and services will yield a well-articulated needs assessment.

The planning committee of a county youth bureau must develop an adequate data base as a part of its data-collection effort. At least four types of data should be collected: (1) quantitative data that identify the level of concentration of youth needs or problems; (2) quantitative and descriptive data that identify types of services and levels of resources to address youth issues, needs, and problems; (3) expert, lay, and consumer opinion critical to youth issues, needs, and problems; and (4) data about program performance as it relates to funding, program development, and systems refinement.

Once data have been collected, the second activity, data analysis, involves the methods and techniques that transfer raw data into information that can be structured for program planners. Statistical analyses of data, demographic interpretations, and qualitative case studies are examples of the kinds of useful data analyses for the youth services planner. Critical to this activity is the principle of relevancy. All data analyses should be completed in such a manner as to be useful for the design of action strategies, the second component of the comprehensive plan.

The needs assessment component is completed with the statement of needs activity. This is a summary of the findings and is critical to the comprehensive planning process. It is at this juncture that the local planners must synthesize their findings, consolidating the data collected from municipal, city, and village perspectives, so as to begin to address youth needs.

Design of Action Strategies

This segment of the Comprehensive Plan is critical, because it is through this component that the youth bureau details how it plans to address the youth needs identified, indicates the level of commitment for the needs identified, and justifies its strategies to meet those needs.

The first activity for the planning committee is to formulate goals and objectives. By definition, a goal is a statement of purpose or ideal that is long range in scope and articulates the policy solution for the needs previously described. An objective is a statement of outcomes that are measurable and observable, that usually progress toward the realization of the goal.

Once goals and objectives are stated, the comprehensive plan requires the development of strategies to achieve them. Strategies for youth services planners in communities fall into three areas: community development/advocacy, coordination/networking, and provision of services. The Comprehensive Plan must articulate each of these areas and describe how each affects the completion of a goal or objective. Thus, community development/advocacy strategies must include such activities as community education and awareness of youth issues, community organizing, and letter writing and telephone campaigns. Those activities that involve community coordination or networking must include integration of services and communication among town, village, and city governance and administrative structures, as well as the private sector. Services may be provided indirectly where the youth bureau contracts with community-based organizations to provide youth programs and services; or directly where the youth bureau provides the services themselves or through other local governmental structures. In either case, the county comprehensive plan must articulate how these services will be provided as a function of its design of action strategies component.

Implementation

The implementation component of the comprehensive planning process includes the specific design of tasks and activities that will be undertaken to ensure that the strategies identified are delivered within the scope of the youth services delivery system. It is a detailed statement of who does what, when, how, and where. It may include narratives, charts, and timelines, all supporting the tasks and activities to be accomplished. To support its plan, the youth bureau should include, as part of the implementation component, the design for an annual progress report, the purpose of which is to discuss accomplishments and refine data, goals, objectives, and action strategies.

Monitoring/Evaluation

The County Comprehensive Plan and the process by which it is developed must also include a description of the manner in which youth services within the municipality will be monitored and evaluated. Monitoring consists of those activities by which a program's ability to provide the services specified in its contract is assessed. Program evaluation consists of activities that assess the contractor's effectiveness in delivering the programs and services it purports to provide to its youth. Monitoring is an attempt to draw conclusions from direct observations, interviews, or physical documentation to certify that the program is performing its contractual obligation. Evaluations are interpretations drawn from program data to ascertain what the program effects are on the youth it serves.

Within the New York state system, there are two levels of monitoring and evaluation activities. At the local and municipal levels, the youth bureaus are responsible for monitoring and evaluating all the programs for which they hold contracts and provide state funding. Thus, information is collected by local public administrators at the local level by local effort. This information is then aggregated and used for statewide policy analysis, program evaluation, and refinement. At the state level, the Division for Youth is responsible for monitoring and evaluating the youth bureau in its activities. Thus, through this two-tiered system, the state public administrator, by monitoring the youth bureaus that receive state aid for their locality (i.e., county or municipality), is in the best position to audit youth bureau monitoring and evaluation activities, as well as be accountable for the state funds provided. At the same time, based upon the knowledge of youth needs and problems as articulated through aggregated information collected in the County Comprehensive Plans, the public administrator is in the best position to appropriate money in order to develop a statewide youth services system of programs.

SUMMARY

In this chapter we provided the background, historical perspectives, development, and models for the public administration of youth programs and services for local communities. The ability of the public administrator to manage the public good through the development of quality youth services, the appropriation of limited resources, and the accountability of structure is a direct result of the manager's sensitivity, openness, skill level in managing resources (both fiscal as well as personnel), willingness to articulate standards, and willingness to advocate in constant and consistent terms with fairness and equity. It is with this delicate balance, in addition to clarity of purpose, mission, role, and function, that the public administrator is able to provide the impetus for quality youth programs to be developed in, for, and by communities.

Chapter 7

Future Perspectives

Three comprehensive evaluations of the effectiveness of Aggression Replacement Training have now been conducted, two with incarcerated youth (Goldstein & Glick, 1987) and the aftercare investigation reported in chapter 5. All three have yielded consistently positive results on both proximal outcome measures, such as prosocial skills acquisition and anger arousal reduction, and more distal criteria, including recidivism and other indices of community functioning. These are highly promising findings, obtained on samples from populations chronically resistant to change. They are findings that encourage two future directions. The first is attempts at replication by investigators other than ourselves. We urge the systematic scrutiny of ART by diverse research teams in diverse settings as necessary tests of the robustness of Aggression Replacement Training and as a precondition to its broader dissemination and utilization.

But interventions are never to be considered set, complete, or final. Interventions designed to alter cognitive-affective-behavioral constellations as complex as juvenile delinquency must constantly be revised, elaborated, extended, and improved. How may Aggression Replacement Training be revised, elaborated, extended, or improved? We suggest two avenues.

Juvenile delinquency has its roots in both the delinquents themselves and the community of which they are a part. A comprehensive intervention must be responsive to both sources. The youth's optimal repertoire of prosocial proficiencies—that is, the collection of competencies that permit him or her to lead a satisfying and effective life without resort to illegal avenues of reward—certainly extends well beyond the three intervention domains that constitute Aggression Replacement Training. In the following section, we describe our attempt to accomplish this elaboration of what may appropriately be offered to delinquent youth in order to substantially enhance their prosocial functioning. Following this presentation, the community is our focus. Here, we describe a comprehensive approach to intervention in the community that goes considerably beyond, but was encouraged by, the apparent value of the parent and sibling groups presented earlier.

THE PREPARE CURRICULUM

Reflecting more comprehensively the competency-enhancing aspiration of Aggression Replacement Training, the Prepare Curriculum (Goldstein, 1988) consists of 10 course-length interventions designed to be used for prosocially deficient youth. Courses are designed to be used in individualized sets and sequences, and rely upon teaching formats and contents selected for their intrinsic motivational attraction for participating youth. Table 7.1 lists the 10-course Prepare Curriculum.

Problem-Solving Training teaches youth how to generate alternative problem solutions, evaluate their relative effectiveness, choose among them, try out the alternative chosen, and determine its adequacy. Problem-Solving Training is presented first, not only for its considerable value as a prosocial skill, but also for its great usefulness as an organizer of decisions about which of the other Prepare course contents to select and employ in any given circumstance. *Interpersonal Skills Training* is simply another term for Structured Learning, described at length in chapter 2. It, too, is ideally presented early in any Prepare sequence, since its constituent skills play a role in certain other Prepare courses. Interpersonal skill deficiencies may occur because the youth does not know the skill and thus must be taught it via this course, or does know it but is not competent in diagnosing when, where, and with whom to use it. *Situation*

Table 7.1.

		The Prepare Curriculum
Course	1	Problem-Solving Training
Course	2	Interpersonal Skills Training
Course	3	Situational Perception Training
Course	4	Anger Control Training
Course	5	Moral Reasoning Training
Course	6	Stress Management Training
Course	7	Empathy Training
Course	8	Recruiting Supportive Models
Course	9	Cooperative Training
Course	10	Understanding and Using Groups

Perception Training teaches such diagnostic skills and thus serves as an important companion course to Interpersonal Skills Training.

Anger Control Training and *Moral Reasoning Training* were described at length earlier. They combine with Interpersonal Skills Training to constitute Aggression Replacement Training. *Stress Management Training* and *Empathy Training* seek to provide the youth with vital skills relevant to the trainee's own emotional world and that of others, respectively. These two courses appear to be valuable in their own right and also to bear importantly on the facilitation of other Prepare courses, especially the three described next.

Recruiting Supportive Models is a means of teaching youth how to seek out, identify, establish a relationship with, and maintain a relationship with prosocially-oriented adult or peer models. It is a course explicitly responsive to the research finding that having at least one such model was a characteristic in a number of studies that differentiated youth from very difficult environments who survived and thrived as they developed from those who succumbed and turned toward disturbed, antisocial, or asocial lives. It is also a course whose contents rely heavily on the lessons of Interpersonal Skills Training. *Cooperation Training* and *Understanding and Using Groups* complete the Prepare Curriculum. Both courses rely heavily on games, simulations, and group activities, all of which often have special motivational appeal to the action-oriented youth who constitute a significant portion of the prepare Curriculum's target trainees.

The Prepare Curriculum is a new and still largely unevaluated extension of the philosophy that underlies Aggression Replacement Training—that diverse psychological competencies can be taught. We are encouraged by the results of our ART evaluation projects that this belief is correct. We hope others will join us in the effort to continue this evaluation process, vis-à-vis both the ART and Prepare curricula.

INTERVENTION IN THE COMMUNITY

A youngster's delinquent behavior most typically has multiple community roots and is influenced by all of the main actors in his or her interpersonal world—peers, parents, classmates, siblings, and others. Each may model antisocial behavior, reward it when it is displayed by others, and show indifference or hostility when prosocial alternatives are employed. For many delinquent youth, schooling in the diverse antisocial proficiencies that constitute delinquency may thus be very much of a "total-immersion" matter, with the lessons, models, and rewards for delinquency being displayed by a great many of these actors a great deal of the time. The youth, in short, may spend most of his or her life as a member of a culture that teaches and reinforces delinquent behavior with great consistency.

To the degree that this scenario is accurate, we assert the corresponding necessity for intervention to also reflect a total immersion strategy. Offering Aggression Replacement Training or even the full Prepare Curriculum to delinquent youth, their parent(s) and their siblings—as in our aftercare study—is a substantial start in this direction, but only a start. What might a total-immersion intervention utilizing all the main actors in the youth's community look like?

One scenario we can envision might have the following features:

1.   A dozen incarcerated, delinquent youth would be selected for project participation.

2.   While incarcerated, they would be constituted into a living unit and reside together in a facility dorm. They would receive ART as a group three times per week.

3.   The 12 participating youth would be released from the facility as a group, and their release would be early—for example after 8 months instead of the typical 12. A revokation penalty arrangement would be established, with specified infractions in the community resulting in being returned to incarceration.

4.   The group would attend the same school and constitute all of the members of a class, thus placing under project control most of their peer associations.

5.   Their teacher would be a project employee.

6.   The group would participate in ART on a daily basis during the school day.

7.   ART would also be provided to members of the youth's families. Two evenings per week would be devoted to these meetings, one for separate parent and sibling ART group meetings, and one joint meeting each week for both family members and the delinquent youth themselves.

8.   Family aides would be employed to work in the home and community with both family members and participating youth, to coordinate services, offer needed support, serve as advocates, and so forth.

9.   Regular weekend activities of a social or educational nature would take place, involving youth, families, and project staff.

10.   With the passage of time, the community of delinquent youth, parents, siblings, teachers, aides, and ART trainers would gradually become more permeable, inviting into its activities more and more people (peers, adults, etc.) and eventually making indistinguishable the community created by the project from the larger community of which the youth is a part and in which he or she must live.

SUMMARY

We have sketched this fictitious plan for total-immersion community intervention to provide a sense of direction. Delinquent behavior typically has deep community roots and strong community support. Serious efforts to alter such behavior must be in, of, and by the community and must be of sufficient potency. Psychological "dabbling" a couple of hours per week, with any intervention, will simply prove inadequate. Any intervention used must surpass in potency the forces it seeks to combat. Total immersion need not take any of the specific forms we have imagined above, but it must be a total immersion. Antisocial behaviors learned in the community must be unlearned in the community; prosocial alternative behaviors to be used in the community must be taught in the community.

References

Adams, S. (1961). *Assessment of the psychiatric treatment program, phase I.* Research Report No. 21, Sacramento, CA: California Youth Authority.

Adams, S. (1962). The PICO Project. In N. Johnson, L. Savitz, & M. E. Wolfgang (Eds.), *The Sociology of Punishment and Correction.* New York: Wiley.

Adkins, W. R. (1974). Life skills: Structured counseling for the disadvantaged. *Personnel and Guidance Journal, 49,* 108–116.

Agee, V. L. (1979). *Treatment of the violent incorrigible adolescent.* Lexington, MA: Lexington Books.

Agras, W. S. (1967). Transfer during systematic desensitization therapy. *Behavior Research and Therapy, 5,* 193–199.

Alexander, J. F., & Parsons, B. V. (1973). Short-term behavioral intervention with delinquent families: Impact on family process and recidivism. *Journal of Abnormal Psychology, 81,* 219–225.

Arbuthnot, J., & Gordon, D. A. (1983). Moral reasoning development in correctional intervention. *Journal of Correctional Education, 34,* 133–138.

Argyle, M., Trower, P., & Bryant, B. (1974). Explorations in the treatment of personality disorders and neurosis by social skill training. *British Journal of Medical Psychology, 47,* 63–72.

Bailey, J. S., Wolf, M. M., & Phillips, E. L. (1970). Home-based reinforcement and the modification of pre-delinquents' classroom behavior. *Journal of Applied Behavior Analysis, 3,* 223–233.

Bartollas, C. (1985). *Correctional treatment: Theory and practice.* Englewood Cliffs, NJ: Prentice-Hall.

Berkowitz, B. P., & Graziano, A. M. (1972). Training parents as behavior therapists: A review. *Behavior Research and Therapy, 10,* 297–317.

Bernstein, K., & Christiansen, K. (1965). A resocialization experiment with short-term offenders. *Scandinavian Studies in Criminology, 1,* 35–54.

Bower, D. G. (1976). *Systems of organization: Management of human resources.* Ann Arbor: University of Michigan Press.

Bright, P. D., & Robin, A. L. (1981). Ameliorating parent-adolescent conflict with problem-solving communication training. *Journal of Behavior Therapy and Experimental Psychiatry, 12,* 275–280.

Brody, S. R. (1978). *The effectiveness of sentencing—A review of the literature.* (Home Offices Research Study #35). London: H.M.S.O.

Brophy, J. (1985). Teachers' expectations, motives, and goals for working with problem students. In C. Ames & R. Ames (Eds.), *Research on motivation in education*, Vol. 2. Orlando, FL: Academic Press, Inc.

California Department of the Youth Authority (1967). James Marshall Treatment Program. In *The statue of current research in the California Youth Authority*. Sacramento, CA: California Youth Authority.

Carney, F. J. (1966). *Summary of studies on the derivation of base expectancy categories for predicting recidivism of subjects released from institutions of the Massachusetts Department of Corrections*. Boston: Massachusetts Department of Corrections.

Center for Studies of Crime and Delinquency (1973). *Community based correctional program models and practices*. Washington, DC: National Institute of Mental Health.

Cohen, H. L., & Filipczak, J. A. (1971). *A new learning environment*. San Francisco: Jossey-Bass.

Craft, M., Stephenson, G., & Granger, C. (1964). A controlled trial of authoritarian and self-governing regimes with adolescent psychopaths. *American Journal of Orthopsychiatry, 34*, 543–554.

Cronbach, L. J., & Snow, R. E. (1977). *Aptitudes and instructional methods*. New York: Irvington Publishers.

Curry, J. F., Wiencrot, S. I., & Koehler, F. (1984). Family therapy with aggressive and delinquent adolescents. In C. R. Keith (Ed.). *The aggressive adolescent*. New York: Free Press.

Davidson, W. S., II, & Seidman, E. (1974). Studies of behavior modification and juvenile delinquency: A review, methodological critique, and social perspective. *Psychological Bulletin, 8*, 998–1011.

Druckman, J. M. (1979). A family-oriented policy and treatment program for female juvenile status offenders. *Journal of Marriage and the Family*, August, 627–636.

Edelman, E., & Goldstein, A. P. (1984). Prescriptive relationship levels for juvenile delinquents in a psychotherapy analog. *Aggressive Behavior, 10*, 269–278.

Elardo, P., & Cooper, M. (1977). *AWARE: Activities for social development*. Reading, MA: Addison-Wesley.

Empey, L. T. (1969). Contemporary programs for convicted juvenile offenders: Problems of theory, practice and research. In D. J. Mulvihill & M. M. Tumin (Eds.), *Crimes of violence*. (Vol. 13), Washington, DC: US Government Printing Office.

Empey, L. T. (1978). *American delinquency: Meaning and construction*. Homewood, LI: Dorsey Press.

Empey, L. T., & Erickson, M. L. (1972). *The Provo experiment: Evaluating community control of delinquency*. Lexington, MA: Lexington Books.

Empey, L. T., & Lubeck, S. G. (1971). *The Silverlake experiment: Testing delinquency theory and community intervention*. Chicago: Aldine.

Fagan, J. A., & Hartstone, E. (1984). Strategic planning in juvenile justice. In R. A. Mathias, P. De Muro, & R. S. Albinson (Eds.), *Violent juvenile offenders*. San Francisco: National Council on Crime and Delinquency.

Farrington, D. P., Ohlin, L. E., & Wilson, J. Q. (1986). *Understanding and controlling crime*. New York: Springer-Verlag.

Feindler, E., & Ecton, R. (1987). *Anger control training*. New York: Pergamon Press.

Feindler, E. L., Marriott, S. A., & Iwata, M. (1984). Group anger control training for junior high school delinquents. *Cognitive Therapy and Research, 8*, 299–311.

Feldman, R. A., Caplinger, T. E., & Wodarski, J. S. (1983). *The St. Louis Conundrum: The Effective Treatment of Antisocial Youths*. Englewood Cliffs, NJ: Prentice-Hall.

Freedman, B. J., Rosenthal, L., Donahoe, C. P., Schlundt, D. G., & McFall, R. M. (1978). Social-behavioral analysis of skill deficits in delinquent and non-delinquent adolescent boys. *Journal of Consulting and Clinical Psychology. 46*, 1448–1462.

Garrity, D. (1956). *The effects of length of incarceration upon parole adjustment and estimation of optimum sentence.* Unpublished doctoral dissertation, University of Washington, Seattle.

Gensheimer, L. K., Mayer, J. P., Gottschalk, R., & Davidson, W. S. (1986). Diverting youth from the Juvenile Justice System: A meta-analysis of intervention efficacy. In S. J. Apter & A. P. Goldstein (Eds.), *Youth violence.* New York: Pergamon Press.

Gibbs, J. C. (1986). Small group sociomoral treatment programs. Dilemmas for use with conduct-disordered or antisocial adolescents or preadolescents. Unpublished manuscript, Ohio State University.

Glaser, D. (1973). The state of the art of criminal justice evaluation. Paper presented at Association for Criminal Justice Research, Los Angeles, November.

Glick, B. (1986). Programming for juvenile delinquents: An administrative perspective. In S. J. Apter & A. P. Goldstein (Eds.), *Youth violence: Programs and prospects.* New York: Pergamon Press.

Goins, S. (1977). The serious or violent juvenile offender—Is there a treatment response? *The Serious Juvenile Offender: Proceedings of a National Symposium.* Washington, DC: Government Printing Office.

Goldstein, A. P. (1973). *Structured learning therapy: Toward a psychotherapy for the poor.* New York: Academic Press.

Goldstein, A. P. (1978). *Prescriptions for child mental health and education.* New York: Pergamon Press.

Goldstein, A. P. (1981). *Psychological Skill Training.* New York: Pergamon Press.

Goldstein, A. P. (1988). *The Prepare Curriculum.* Champaign, IL: Research Press.

Goldstein, A. P., & Glick, B. (1987). *Aggression Replacement Training.* Champaign, IL: Research Press.

Goldstein, A. P., & Kanfer, F. (1979). *Maximizing treatment gains.* New York: Academic Press.

Goldstein, A. P., & Stein, N. (1976). *Prescriptive psychotherapies.* New York: Pergamon Press.

Goldstein, A. P., Apter, S. J., & Harootunian, B. (1984). *School violence.* Englewood Cliffs, NJ: Prentice-Hall.

Goldstein, A. P., Keller, H., & Erne, D. (1985). *Changing the abusive parent.* Champaign, IL: Research Press.

Goldstein, A. P., Sherman, M., Gershaw, N. J., Sprafkin, R. P., & Glick, B. (1978). Training aggressive adolescents in prosocial behavior. *Journal of Youth and Adolescence, 7,* 73–92.

Goldstein, A. P., Sprafkin, R. P., Gershaw, N. J., & Klein, P. (1979). *Skillstreaming the adolescent.* Urbana: Research Press.

Gottschalk, R., Davidson, W. S., Gensheimer, L. K., & Mayer, J. P. (1987). Community-based interventions. In H. C. Quay (Ed.), *Handbook of juvenile delinquency.* New York: Wiley.

Grant, J., & Grant, M. Q. (1959). A group dynamics approach to the treatment of nonconformists in the navy. *Annals of the American Academy of Political and Social Science, 322,* 126–135.

Gruber, R. P. (1971). Behavior therapy: Problems in generalization. *Behavior Therapy, 2,* 361–368.

Guerney, B. G. (1977). *Relationship enhancement.* San Francisco: Jossey-Bass.

Hargardine, J. E. (1968). *The Attention Homes of Boulder, Colorado.* Juvenile Delinquency and Youth Development Office, U.S. Department of Health, Education and Welfare, Washington, DC.

Hare, M. A. (1976). *Teaching conflict resolution situations.* Paper presented at Eastern Community Association, Philadelphia.

Harlow, E., Weber, J. R., & Wilkins, L. T. (1971). *Community based correctional program models and practices.* Washington, DC: National Institute of Mental Health, Center for Studies of Crime and Delinquency.

Harrison, R. M., & Mueller, P. (1964). *Clue hunting about group counseling and parole outcome.* Sacramento, CA: California Department of Corrections.

Hawley, R. C., & Hawley, I. L. (1975). *Developing human potential: A handbook of activities for personal and social growth.* Amherst, MA: Educational Research Associates.

Heiman, H. (1973). Teaching interpersonal communications. *North Dakota Speech and Theatre Association Bulletin, 2,* 7–29.

Heller, K., Price, R. H., Reinharz, S., Riger, S. & Wandersman, A., & D'Aunno, T. A. (1984). *Psychology and community change.* Homewood, IL: Dorsey Press.

Hoshmand, L. T., & Austin, G. W. (1987). Validation studies of a multifactor cognitive-behavioral anger control inventory. *Journal of Personality Assessment, 51,* 417–432.

Hoshmand, L. T., Austin, G. W., & Appell, J. (1981). *The diagnosis and assessment of anger control problems.* Paper presented at American Psychological Association, August, New York City.

Hunt, D. E. (1972). Matching models for teacher training. In B. R. Joyce & M. Weil (Eds.), *Perspectives for reform in teacher education.* Englewood Cliffs, NJ: Prentice-Hall.

Jesness, C. F. (1965). *The Fricot Ranch Study.* Sacramento, CA: California Department of the Youth Authority.

Karoly, P., & Steffan, J. (1980). *Improving the long term effects of psychotherapy.* New York: Guilford Press.

Kazdin, A. E., & Frame, C. (1983). Aggressive behavior and conduct disorders. In R. J. Morris & T. R. Kratochwill (Eds.), *The practice of child therapy.* New York: Pergamon Press, 167–192.

Keeley, S. M., Shemberg, K. M., & Carbonell, J. (1976). Operant clinical intervention: Behavior management or beyond? Where are the data? *Behavior Therapy, 7,* 292–305.

Keith, C. R. (Ed.) (1984). *The aggressive adolescent.* New York: Free Press.

Keller, F. S. (1966). A personal course in psychology. In R. Uluch, T. Stachnik, & J. Mabry (Eds.), *Control of human behavior.* Glenview, IL: Scott, Foresman & Co.

Keller, H., Goldstein, A. P., & Wynn, R. (1988). *Aggression prevention training.* Unpublished manuscript, Syracuse University.

Kentucky Child Welfare Research Foundation (1967). Community Rehabilitation of the Younger Delinquent Boy: Parkland Non-Residential Group Center, U.S. Department of Health, Education and Welfare.

Kiesler, D. J. (1969). A grid model for the psychotherapies. In L. D. Eron & R. Callahan (Eds.), *The relation of theory to practice in psychotherapy.* Chicago: Aldine.

Kifer, R E., Lewis, M. A., Green, D. R., & Phillips, E. L. (1974). Training predelinquent youth and their parents to negotiate conflict situations. *Journal of Applied Behavior Analysis, 7,* 357–364.

Klausmeier, H. J., Rossmiller, R. A., & Saily, M. (1977). *Individually guided elementary education.* New York: Academic Press.

Knight, D. (1969). *The Marshall Program: Assessment of a short-term institutional treatment program.* Research Report No. 56, Sacramento, CA: California Youth Authority.

Kohlberg, L. (1969). Stage and sequence: The cognitive-developmental approach to socialization. In D. A. Goslin (Ed.), *Handbook of socialization theory and research.* Chicago: Rand McNally.

Kohlberg, L. (Ed.) (1973). *Collected papers on moral development and moral education.* Cambridge, MA: Center for Moral Education, Harvard University.

Krasner, L. (Ed.). (1980). *Environmental design and human behavior: A psychology of the individual in society.* New York: Pergamon Press.

Lavin, G. K., Trabka, S., & Kahn, E. M. (1984). Group therapy with aggressive and delinquent adolescents. In C. R. Keith (Ed.), *The aggressive adolescent.* New York: Free Press.

Likert, R. (1967). *The human organization.* New York: McGraw-Hill.

Lundman, R. J. (1984). *Prevention and control of delinquency.* New York: Oxford University Press.

Magaro, P. A. (1969). A prescriptive treatment model based upon social class and premorbid adjustment. *Psychotherapy: Theory, Research and Practice, 6,* 57–70.

Maltz, M. D. (1984). *Recidivism.* New York: Academic Press.

Martinson, R. (1974). What works? Questions and answers about prison reform. *The Public Interest,* Spring: 22–54.

Mayer, J. P., Gensheimer, L. K., Davidson, W. S., & Gottschalk, R. (1986). Social learning treatment within juvenile justice: A meta-analysis of impact in the natural environment. In S. J. Apter & A. P. Goldstein (Eds.), *Youth violence: Programs and prospects.* New York: Pergamon Press.

McCorkle, L., Elias, A., & Bixby, F. (1958). *The Highfields story: A unique experiment in the treatment of juvenile delinquency.* New York: Holt.

McGinnis, E., & Goldstein, A. P. (1984). *Skillstreaming the elementary school child.* Champaign, IL: Research Press.

Meichenbaum, D. (1977). *Cognitive behavior modification: An integrative approach.* New York: Plenum.

Merrill-Palmer Institute (1971). *The Detroit Foster Home Project,* Unpublished manuscript, Detroit, MI.

Moos, R. H., & Insel, B. (1974). *Family environment scale, Form R.* Palo Alto, CA: Consulting Psychologists Press.

Northern California Service League (1968). *Final report of the San Francisco Rehabilitation Project for Offenders,* San Francisco.

Novaco, R. W. (1975). *Anger control: The development and evaluation of an experimental treatment.* Lexington, MA: Lexington.

O'Dell, S. (1974). Training parents in behavior modification: A review. *Psychological Bulletin, 81,* 418–433.

Palmer, T. B. (1973). Matching worker and client in corrections. *Social Work, 18,* 95–103.

Palmer, T. (1975). Martinson revisited. *Journal of Research in Crime and Delinquency, 12,* 133–152.

Parsons, B. V., & Alexander, J. F. (1973). Short-term family intervention: A therapy outcome study. *Journal of Consulting and Clinical Psychology, 41,* 195–201.

Patterson, G. R. (1971). Behavioral intervention procedures in the classroom and in the home. In A. E. Bergin & S. L. Garfield (Eds.), *Handbook of psychotherapy on behavior change.* New York: Wiley.

Patterson, G. R. (1974). Interventions for boys with conduct problems: Multiple settings, treatments, and criteria. *Journal of Consulting and Clinical Psychology, 42,* 471–481.

Patterson, G. R. (1976). The aggressive child: Victim and architect of a coercive system. In L. A. Hamerlynck, L. C. Handy, & E. J. Mash (Eds.), *Behavior modification and families: Theory and research.* New York: Bruner/Mazel.

Patterson, G. R. (1979). Treatment for children with conduct problems: A review of outcome studies. In S. Feshbach & A. Fraczek (Eds.), *Aggression and behavior change: Biological and social processes.* New York: Praeger.

Patterson, G. R., Reid, J. G., Jones, R. R., & Conger, R. E. (1975). *A Social learning approach to family intervention.* Eugene, OR: Catalia.

Pawlicki, R. (1970). Behaviour therapy research with children: A critical review. *Canadian Journal of Behavioral Science, 2,* 163–173.

Phillips, E. L. (1968). Achievement Place: Token reinforcement procedures in a home style rehabilitation setting for predelinquent boys. *Journal of Applied Behavior Analysis, 7,* 207–215.

Plas, J. M. (1986). *Systems psychology in the schools.* New York: Pergamon Press.

Pond, E. M. (1968). A comparative study of the Community Delinquency Control Project.

In *The Status of Current Research in the California Youth Authority*, Sacramento, CA: California Youth Authority.

Post, G. C., Hicks, R. A., & Monfort, M. F. (1968). Day care program for delinquents: A new treatment approach. *Crime and Delinquency, 14*, 353–359.

Redner, R., Snellman, L, & Davidson, W. S. (1983). In R. J. Morris & T. R. Kratochwill (Eds.), *The practice of child therapy*, New York: Pergamon, 193–220.

Robin, A. L. (1983). Parent-adolescent conflict: A developmental problem of families. *Proceedings of the Fifteenth Banff Conference on Behavior Science. Banff, Alberta.*

Robin, L., Kent, R., O'Leary, D., Foster, S., & Prinz, R. (1977). An approach to teaching parents and adolescents problem-solving communication skills: A preliminary report. *Behavior Therapy, 8*, 639–643.

Romig, D. A. (1978). *Justice for our children: An examination of Juvenile Delinquency Rehabilitation Programs*. Lexington, MA: Lexington Books.

Rutter, M., & Giller, H. (1983). *Juvenile delinquency: Trends & perspectives*. New York: Guilford Press.

Sealy, A., & Banks, C. (1971). Social maturity, training, experience, and recidivism amongst British borstal boys. *British Journal of Criminology, 11*, 245–264.

Serna, L. A., Schumaker, J. B., Hazel, J. S., & Sheldon, J. B. (1986). Teaching reciprocal social sills to parents and their delinquent adolescents. *Journal of Clinical Child Psychology, 15*, 64–77.

Slavson, S. R. (1964). *A textbook of analytic group psychotherapy*. New York: International Universities Press.

Sloop, E. W. (1975). Parents as behavior modifiers. In W. D. Gentry (Ed.), *Applied behavior modification*. St. Louis: Mosby.

Snyder, J., & Patterson, G. (1987). Family interaction and delinquent behavior. In H. C. Quay (Ed.). *Handbook of juvenile delinquency*. New York: Wiley.

Spence, S. H. (1981). Differences in social skills performance between institutionalized juvenile male offenders and a comparable group of boys without offense records. *British Journal of Clinical Psychology, 20*, 163–171.

Stark, H. (1967). Alternatives to institutionalization. *Crime and delinquency, 13*, 323–329.

Staub, E. (1979). *Positive social behavior and morality, Vol. 2*. New York: Academic Press.

Stein, N., & Bogin, D. (1978). Individual child psychotherapy. In A. P. Goldstein (Ed.), *Prescriptions for child mental health and education*. New York: Pergamon Press.

Stephens, T. M. (1976). *Social Skills in the Classroom*. Columbus, OH: Cedars Press.

Stephenson, R. M., & Scarpitti, F. R. (1969). Essexfields: A nonresidential experiment in group centered rehabilitation of delinquents. *American Journal of Correction, 31*, 12–18.

Terrance, M. (1971). *Positive Action for Youth* (PAY). Mott Crime and Delinquency Prevention Program, Flint Board of Education, Flint, Michigan.

Tharp, R. G., & Wetzel, R. J. (1969). *Behavior modification in the natural environment*. New York: Academic Press.

Urwick, L. F. (1955). The Purpose of Business. *Dun's Review and Modern Industry, 52*, 103–105.

Urwick, L. F. (1961). Management and Human Relations. In R. Tannenbaum (Ed.), *Leadership and organization: A Behavior Science Approach*, 118–131. New York: McGraw-Hill.

U.S. Department of Justice (1977). *Project New Pride*, National Institute of Law Enforcement and Criminal Justice. Washington, D.C.: Government Printing Office.

Vorrath, H., & Brendtro, L. K. (1974). *Positive peer culture*. Chicago: Aldine.

Warren, M. Q. (1966). *Interpersonal maturity level classification*. Sacramento, CA: California Youth Authority.

Warren, M. Q. (1974). *Classification for treatment*. Presented at Seminar on the Classification of Criminal Behavior, Washington, DC: National Institute of Law Enforcement and Criminal Justice.

Weathers, L., & Liberman, R. P. (1975). Contingency contracting with families of delinquent adolescents. *Behavior Therapy, 6,* 356–366.

Wilkins, L. T., & Gottfredson, D. M. (1969). *Research, demonstration and social action.* National Council on Crime and Delinquency, Davis, California.

Woodson, R. L. (1981). *A summons to life: Mediating structures and the prevention of youth crime.* Cambridge, MA: Ballinger.

Wright, W. E., & Dixon, M. C. (1977). Community prevention and treatment of juvenile delinquency: A review of evaluation studies. *Journal of Research in Crime and Delinquency, 14,* 35–67.

Zimmerman, D. (1983). Moral education. In Center for Research on Aggression (Ed.), *Prevention and control of aggression.* New York: Pergamon, 210–240.

Author Index

Adams, S., 8, 118
Adkins, W.R., 18, 118
Agee, V.L., 11, 118
Agras, W.S., 21, 118
Albinson, R.S., 119
Alexander, J.F., 14, 118, 122
Ames, C., 118
Ames, R., 118
Appell, J., 86, 121
Apter, S.J., 12, 119, 120, 122
Arbuthnot, J., 29, 118
Argyle, M., 18, 118
Auston, G.W., 86, 121

Bailey, J.S., 13, 118
Banks, C., 9, 10, 123
Bartillas, C., 6, 118
Bergin, A.E., 122
Berkowitz, B.P., 13, 118
Bernstein, K., 9, 118
Bixby, F., 8, 121
Blatt, M., 42
Bogin, D., 8, 123
Bower, D.G., 96, 118
Brendtro, L.K., 8, 123
Bright, P.D., 118
Brody, S.R., 4
Brophy, J., 54, 118
Bryant, B., 18, 118

California Department of Youth Authority, 2, 3, 8, 10, 119
Callahan, R., 121
Caplinger, T.E., 1, 4, 119

Carbonell, J., 25, 121
Carney, F.J., 8, 119
Center for Research on Aggression, 123
Center for Studies of Crime and Delinquency, 4, 119
Christiansen, K., 9, 118
Cohen, H.L., 3, 119
Colby, A., 42
Conger, R.E., 17, 122
Cooper, M., 18, 119
Craft, M., 8, 9, 119
Cronbach, L.J., 8, 119
Curry, J.F., 9, 119

D'Aunno, T.A., 12
Davidson, W.S., II, 5, 9, 10, 119, 120, 122
De Muro, P., 119
Dixon, M.C., 4, 123
Donohoe, C.P., 17
Druckman, J.M., 90, 119

Ecton, R., 25, 119
Edelman, E., 11, 119
Elardo, P., 18, 119
Elias, A., 8, 121
Empey, L.T., 3, 9, 10, 95, 119
Erickson, M.L., 3, 119
Erne, D., 60, 120
Eron, L.D., 121

Fagan, J.A., 4, 119
Farrington, D.P., 86, 119
Feindler, E.L., 25, 119
Feldman, R.A., 1, 4, 5, 119

Feshbach, S., 122
Filipczak, J.A., 3, 119
Foster, S., 14, 122
Fraczek, A., 122
Frame, C., 13, 121
Freedman, B.J., 17

Garfield, S.L., 122
Garrity, D., 9, 10, 119
Gensheimer, L.K., 5, 9, 10, 119, 120, 122
Gentry, W.D., 123
Gershaw, N.J., 24, 85, 120
Gibbs, J.C., 28, 119
Giller, H., 4, 123
Glaser, D., 9, 120
Glick, B., 7, 24, 80, 81, 96, 97, 113, 120
Goins, S., 4, 120
Goldstein, A.P., 7, 8, 11, 12, 18, 24, 25,
    60, 64, 80, 81, 85, 97, 113, 114, 119,
    120, 121, 122
Gordon, D.A., 29, 118
Goslin, D.A., 121
Gottfredson, D.M., 3, 123
Gottschalk, R., 5, 9, 10, 119, 120, 122
Granger, C., 8, 119
Grant, J., 10, 120
Grant, M.Q., 10, 120
Graziano, A.M., 13, 118
Green, D.R., 14, 121
Gruber, R.P., 21, 120
Guerney, B.Q., 18, 120

Hamerlynck, L.A., 122
Handy, L.C., 122
Hare, M.A., 18, 120
Hargardine, J.R., 3, 120
Harlow, E., 3, 6, 120
Harootunian, B., 12, 120
Harrison, R.M., 8, 120
Hartstone, E., 4, 119
Hawley, I.L., 18, 120
Hawley, R.C., 18, 120
Hazel, J.S., 14, 123
Heiman, H., 18, 120
Heller, K., 12, 120
Hicks, R.A., 3, 122
Hoshmand, L.T., 86, 121
Hunt, D.E., 8, 121

Insel, B., 12, 86, 122
Iwata, M., 25, 119

Jesness, C.F., 9, 121
Johnson, N., 118
Jones, R.R., 17, 122
Joyce, B.R., 121

Kahn, E.M., 9, 121
Kanfer, F., 24, 25, 120
Karoly, P., 24, 25, 121
Kazdin, A.E., 13, 121
Keeley, S.M., 25, 121
Keith, C.R., 9, 119, 121
Keller, F.S., 64, 121
Keller, H., 8, 60, 120, 121
Kent, R., 14, 122
Kentucky Child Welfare Research Founda-
    tion, 3, 121
Kiesler, D.J., 8, 121
Kifer, R.E., 14, 121
Klausmeier, H.J., 8, 121
Klein, P., 24, 85, 120
Knight, D., 8, 9, 121
Koehler, F., 9, 119
Kohlberg, L., 28, 121
Krasner, L., 12, 121
Kratochwill, T.R., 121, 122

Lavin, G.K., 9, 121
Lewis, M.A., 14, 121
Liberman, R.P., 14, 123
Likert, R., 96, 121
Lubeck, S.G., 3, 119
Lundman, R.J., 6,121

Magaro, P.A., 8, 121
Maltz, M.D., 122
Marriott, S.A., 25, 119
Martinson, R., 4, 7, 122
Mash, E.J., 122
Mathias, R.A., 199
Mayer, J.P., 5, 9, 10, 119, 120, 122
McCorkle, L., 8, 121
McFall, R.M., 17
McGinnis, E., 64, 121
Meichenbaum, D., 25, 122
Merrill-Palmer Institute, 3, 122
Monfort, M.F., 3, 122
Moos, R.H., 12, 86, 122
Morris, R.J., 121, 122
Mueller, P., 8, 120
Mulvihill, D.J., 119

Northern California Service Leauge, 3, 122
Novaco, R.W., 25, 122

O'Dell, S., 13, 122
Ohlin, L.E., 86, 119
O'Leary, D., 14, 122

Palmer, T.B., 7, 10, 122
Parsons, B.V., 14, 118, 122
Patterson, G.R., 14, 15, 17, 122, 123
Pawlicki, R., 13, 122
Phillips, E.L., 3, 13, 14, 118, 121, 122
Plas, J.M., 12, 122
Pond, E.M., 2, 122
Post, G.C., 3, 122
Price, R.H., 12, 120
Prinz, R., 14, 122

Redner, R., 9, 122
Reid, J.G., 17, 122
Reinharz, S., 12, 120
Riger, S., 12, 120
Robin, A.L., 14, 118, 122
Robin, L., 122
Romig, D.A., 4, 123
Rosenthal, L., 17
Rossmiller, R.A., 8, 121
Rutter, M., 4, 123

Saily, M., 8, 121
Savitz, L., 118
Scarpitti, F.R., 3, 123
Schlundt, D.G., 17
Schumaker, J.B., 14, 123
Sealy, A., 9, 10, 123
Seidman, E., 9, 119
Serna, L.A., 14, 123
Sheldon, J.B., 14, 123
Shemberg, K.M., 25, 121
Sherman, M., 24, 120
Slavson, S.R., 8, 123
Sloop, E.W., 13, 123

Snellman, L., 9, 122
Snow, R.E., 8, 119
Snyder, J., 15, 123
Sprafkin, R.P., 24, 85, 120
Speicher, B., 42
Spence, S.H., 17, 123
Stark, H., 2, 123
Staub, E., 54, 123
Steffan, J., 24, 25, 121
Stein, N., 7, 8, 120, 123
Stephens, T.M., 18, 123
Stephenson, G., 3, 8, 119
Stephenson, R.M., 123

Tannenbaum, R., 123
Terrance, M., 123
Tharp, R.G., 21, 123
Trabka, S., 9, 121
Trower, P., 18, 118
Tumin, M.M., 119

Urwick, L.F., 123
U.S. Department of Justice, 4, 123

Vorrath, H. 8, 123

Wandersman, A., 12, 120
Warren, M.Q., 8, 9, 120
Weathers, L., 14, 123
Weber, J.R., 3, 120
Weil, M., 121
Wetzel, R.J., 21, 123
Wiencrot, S.I., 9, 119
Wilkins, L.T., 3, 120, 123
Wilson, J.Q., 86, 119
Wodarski, J.S., 1, 4, 119
Wolf, M.M., 13, 118
Wolfgang, M.E., 118
Woodson, R.L., 4, 123
Wright, W.E., 4, 123
Wynn, R., 64, 121

Zimmerman, D., 29, 123

Subject Index

Administration:
  community involvement, 99
  historical development, 94–95
  management theories, 96–98
  networking, 99
  roles and responsibilities, 99–101
  state models, 101–112
  youth participation, 99
Aggression, multiple causes of, 12
Aggression Replacement Training, 17–30
  and Anger Control Training, 15–18
  curriculum, 82–84
  family program, 60–79
  and Moral Education, 28–29
  program evaluation, 80–93
  and Psychological Skill Training, 18–24
  youth program, 31–59
Anger Control Training, 25–28, 39–42
  hassle log, 26
Anger Situation Inventory, 87, 89–90
Community-based evaluation, 81–93
  assessment, 85–87
  design, 81–85
  results, 87–93
Community-based intervention, 1–15,
  115–116
  administration of, 94–112
  historical development, 94–95
  management theories, 96–98
Community-based programs, 2–6
Family Program, 60–79
  facilitators, 62–63
  group building, 75–79
  recruitment for, 64–70

session excerpts, 70–74
  setting, 61
  supports for, 64
Hassle Log, 26
Homework Report, 23
Management theories, 96–98
Modeling, 18
Moral Education, 28–29, 42–46
Motivation, 46–49
  participation, 49–53
  prosocial, 53–56
New York State Division for Youth,
  103–112
Parent training programs, 13–15
Performance feedback, 19
Prepare Curriculum, 114
Prescriptive programming, 7–11
Program evaluation, 80–93
  community-based investigation, 81–9
  earlier investigations, 80–81
Psychological Skill Training, 18–24
  efficacy evaluations of, 24
  Homework Report, 23
  modeling component, 18
  performance feedback component,
  report playing component, 19
  skill curriculum of, 21–23
  transfer of training component, 20–21
Recidivism, 90–93
Role playing, 19
Skill Checklist, 88–89
Structured Learning Skills, 22
Systems intervention, 11–15
Transfer of training, 20–21

Youth Program, 31–59
  attendance motivation, 46–49
  participants, 31–32
  participation motivation, 49–53
  prosocial motivation, 53–56
  setting, 32–33
  session excerpts, 33–46
  trainer lessons, 56–59

About the Authors

Arnold P. Goldstein, Ph.D. (Pennsylvania State University, 1959), joined the clinical psychology section of Syracuse University's Psychology Department in 1963 and both taught there and directed its Psychotherapy Center until 1980. In 1981, he founded the Center for Research on Aggression, which he currently directs. He joined Syracuse University's Division of Special Education in 1985. Professor Goldstein has a career-long interest, as both researcher and practitioner, in difficult-to-reach clients. Since 1980, his main research and psychoeducational focus has been incarcerated juvenile offenders and child-abusing parents. He is the developer of Structured Learning, a psychoeducational program and curriculum designed to teach prosocial behaviors to chronically antisocial persons. Professor Goldstein's books include *Structured Learning Therapy: Toward a Psychotherapy for the Poor, Skill Training for Community Living, Skillstreaming the Adolescent, School Violence, Aggressless, Police Crisis Intervention, Hostage, Prevention and Control of Aggression, Aggression in Global Perspective, In Response to Aggression,* and *Youth Violence,* and *Aggression Replacement Training.*

Barry Glick received his Ph.D. from Syracuse University in 1972. Trained as a counseling psychologist, Dr. Glick has devoted his professional career to the development of policies, programs, and services for adolescents. His specialization is in juvenile delinquency as well as the emotionally disturbed adolescent. Dr. Glick has worked both in private child care agencies and in state government. He has held positions as a child care worker, a psychologist, an administrator and a manager. He currently is Associate Deputy Director of Local Services, New York State Division for Youth. Dr. Glick is certified by the National Board of Certified Counselors and holds membership in a number of professional organizations. He is co-author of *Aggression Replacement Training.*

Mary Jane Irwin is a certified social worker currently serving as assistant director of Hillside Children's Center of Central New York in Syracuse, NY. Her career has included work in public health, low income housing and foster care. She has taught communication skills at Syracuse University and has done consulting in conflict management throughout the United States. Ms. Irwin received her BS & MSW degrees from Syracuse University.

Claudia Pask-McCartney has an M.S. in Counseling, an M.S. in Instructional Development, and is currently a PhD. Candidate in Syracuse University's Department of Instructional Design, Development and Evaluation. She teaches management courses in both the business and mental health fields, conducts program evaluation research and conducts workshops specializing in personal and organizational motivation, communication and conflict management.

Ibrahim S Rubama is a New York State Division for Youth worker in community Care. He has been trained as an economist, political scientist, and gerontologist. Mr. Rubana has been on faculties of Syracuse University and State University of New York at Upstate Medical Center. He has published on community development, advocacy issues, cultural mediation, housing, health, and youth media. He has administered a number of international development projects and consulted for UNESCO, UN, Syracuse University Research Corporation, Literacy Volunteers of America and other agencies.

Psychology Practitioner Guidebooks

Editors
Arnold P. Goldstein, Syracuse University
Leonard Krasner, Stanford University & SUNY at Stony Brook
Sol L. Garfield, Washington University in St. Louis

Elsie M. Pinkston & Nathan L. Linsk—CARE OF THE ELDERLY:
A Family Approach

Donald Meichenbaum—STRESS INOCULATION TRAINING

Sebastiano Santostefano—COGNITIVE CONTROL THERAPY WITH
CHILDREN AND ADOLESCENTS

Lillie Weiss, Melanie Katzman & Sharlene Wolchik—TREATING BULIMIA:
A Psychoeducational Approach

Edward B. Blanchard & Frank Andrasik—MANAGEMENT OF CHRONIC
HEADACHES: A Psychological Approach

Raymond G. Romanczyk—CLINICAL UTILIZATION OF
MICROCOMPUTER TECHNOLOGY

Philip H. Bornstein & Marcy T. Bornstein—MARITAL THERAPY:
A Behavioral-Communications Approach

Michael T. Nietzel & Ronald C. Dillehay—PSYCHOLOGICAL
CONSULTATION IN THE COURTROOM

Elizabeth B. Yost, Larry E. Beutler, M. Anne Corbishley & James R.
Allender—GROUP COGNITIVE THERAPY: A Treatment Approach for
Depressed Older Adults

Lillie Weiss—DREAM ANALYSIS IN PSYCHOTHERAPY

Edward A. Kirby & Liam K. Grimley—UNDERSTANDING AND
TREATING ATTENTION DEFICIT DISORDER

Jon Eisenson—LANGUAGE AND SPEECH DISORDERS IN CHILDREN

Eva L. Feindler & Randolph B. Ecton—ADOLESCENT ANGER
CONTROL: Cognitive-Behavioral Techniques

Michael C. Roberts—PEDIATRIC PSYCHOLOGY: Psychological
Interventions and Strategies for Pediatric Problems

Daniel S. Kirschenbaum, William G. Johnson & Peter M. Stalonas, Jr.—
TREATING CHILDHOOD AND ADOLESCENT OBESITY

W. Stewart Agras—EATING DISORDERS: Management of Obesity,
Bulimia and Anorexia Nervosa

Ian H. Gotlib & Catherine A. Colby—TREATMENT OF DEPRESSION:
An Interpersonal Systems Approach

Walter B. Pryzwansky & Robert N. Wendt—PSYCHOLOGY AS A
PROFESSION: Foundations of Practice

Cynthia D. Belar, William W. Deardorff & Karen E. Kelly—THE
PRACTICE OF CLINICAL HEALTH PSYCHOLOGY

Paul Karoly & Mark P. Jensen—MULTIMETHOD ASSESSMENT OF
CHRONIC PAIN

William L. Golden, E. Thomas Dowd & Fred Friedberg—
HYPNOTHERAPY: A Modern Approach

Patricia Lacks—BEHAVIORAL TREATMENT FOR PERSISTENT INSOMNIA

Arnold P. Goldstein & Harold Keller—AGGRESSIVE BEHAVIOR: Assessment and Intervention

C. Eugene Walker, Barbara L. Bonner & Keith L. Kaufman— THE PHYSICALLY AND SEXUALLY ABUSED CHILD: Evaluation and Treatment

Robert E. Becker, Richard G. Heimberg & Alan S. Bellack—SOCIAL SKILLS TRAINING TREATMENT FOR DEPRESSION

Richard F. Dangel & Richard A. Polster—TEACHING CHILD MANAGEMENT SKILLS

Albert Ellis, John F. McInerney, Raymond DiGiuseppe & Raymond Yeager—RATIONAL-EMOTIVE THERAPY WITH ALCOHOLICS AND SUBSTANCE ABUSERS

Johnny L. Matson & Thomas H. Ollendick—ENHANCING CHILDREN'S SOCIAL SKILLS: Assessment and Training

Edward B. Blanchard, John E. Martin & Patricia M. Dubbert—NON-DRUG TREATMENTS FOR ESSENTIAL HYPERTENSION

Samuel M. Turner & Deborah C. Beidel—TREATING OBSESSIVE-COMPULSIVE DISORDER

Alice W. Pope, Susan M. McHale & W. Edward Craighead—SELF-ESTEEM ENHANCEMENT WITH CHILDREN AND ADOLESCENTS

Jean E. Rhodes & Leonard A. Jason—PREVENTING SUBSTANCE ABUSE AMONG CHILDREN AND ADOLESCENTS

Gerald D. Oster, Janice E. Caro, Daniel R. Eagen & Margaret A. Lillo— ASSESSING ADOLESCENTS

Robin C. Winkler, Dirck W. Brown, Margaret van Keppel & Amy Blanchard—CLINICAL PRACTICE IN ADOPTION

Roger Poppen—BEHAVIORAL RELAXATION TRAINING AND ASSESSMENT

Michael D. LeBow—ADULT OBESITY THERAPY

Robert Paul Liberman, William J. DeRisi & Kim T. Mueser—SOCIAL SKILLS TRAINING FOR PSYCHIATRIC PATIENTS

Johnny L. Matson—TREATING DEPRESSION IN CHILDREN AND ADOLESCENTS

Sol L. Garfield—THE PRACTICE OF BRIEF PSYCHOTHERAPY

Arnold P. Goldstein, Barry Glick, Mary Jane Irwin, Claudia Pask-McCartney & Ibrahim Rubama—REDUCING DELINQUENCY: Intervention in the Community